Rebel

Rebel

My Life Outside the Lines

Nick Nolte

HARPER LUXE

An Imprint of HarperCollinsPublishers

REBEL. Copyright © 2018 by Kingsgate Films, Inc. All rights reserved. Printed in the United States of America. No part of this book may be used or reproduced in any manner whatsoever without written permission except in the case of brief quotations embodied in critical articles and reviews. For information address HarperCollins Publishers, 195 Broadway, New York, NY 10007.

HarperCollins books may be purchased for educational, business, or sales promotional use. For information please e-mail the Special Markets Department at SPsales@harpercollins.com.

FIRST HARPERLUXE EDITION

HarperLuxe™ is a trademark of HarperCollins Publishers

Library of Congress Cataloging-in-Publication Data is available upon request.

ISBN: 978-0-06-229251-3

18 19 20 21 22   ID/LSC   10 9 8 7 6 5 4 3 2 1

To Sophie and Brawley

Contents

The only people who ever called me a rebel were the people who wanted me to do what they wanted.

—NICK NOLTE

We act to save our lives every day.

—MARLON BRANDO

Rebel

Prologue

L et me tell you about my testicle tuck. After the success of *The Prince of Tides*, I decided that I couldn't just sit on my assets and let things succumb to gravity. The procedure was the latest in Hollywood plastic surgery and I was all for it. So, I decided to make the investment. Well, at least that's what I told *Good Morning America* one lovely spring day in 1991. Immediately they said, "Say, 'Good morning, America, Nick,'" and we were off the air. Caught.

It has been said that I lie to the press, that I make up outlandish stories to protect myself. Many accuse me of telling falsehoods just for the sheer joy of pranking. Looking back, I can see a morsel of truth in both. I've tried not to fudge. Part of the impulse could be attributed to my deep shyness amidst a tabloid-driven industry. Fame is a false high. It's not a real place. It's fake. When it's tested, it fails. There's no security in the fame at all. And if you believe in it, it turns out very badly, because it has no substance for you to believe in. So, maybe I find it fun to play on the absurdity of fame. Or maybe I just rebel with a little lie.

A memoir offers the opportunity to tell your story *your* way. I have control over how I tell the story. This appeals to me. Unfortunately, my best intentions may be trounced by a rose-colored reckoning. I've never been any good at real life. Those closest to me would no doubt agree. And my old friend anxiety lurks like a latent virus. I suppose there was ample evidence in my childhood to predict a bumpy ride, but I was twenty-one before I debunked the first of many stories in my life—the story of who I thought I was and what the world was about.

The only place to start this story is at the end of another one. I had a breakthrough. It was the kind of event people watching from the sidelines would call a breakdown. Crack-up. But I saw it as a self-inflicted coming-of-age ritual and one of the best things to happen to me. Those familiar with the insect that undergoes a process of metamorphosis into a flying creature may understand what the hell I'm talking about. Pardon the tired-out metaphor, but it's exactly what happened to me. I was in a chrysalis.

A crack in my veneer let the truth out. My real tale spirals out from there, shedding fictions and building new skins. This is where I start my story. A peek at the corn-fed, ill-equipped young man I was prior to the breakthrough. I was caught in my own act, woven from the stories and identity I inherited. Only the little room in Phoenix could help me get free. And God knows, there's no one to be but yourself after that. You're either renewed or you're dead. And I wasn't ready to be dead. I wanted to act.

Chapter 1
Younger Brother

There was a crash and then a woman yelling. I ran upstairs through throngs of artists and jazz musicians, all the while following a cascading stream of water that led me to the bathroom. The door was open and my roommate Jeanie was on the floor, next to a broken sink, and her lover was pulling his pants up. She had apparently been sitting on it when his insistent thrusts brought it smashing to the floor. Everyone was laughing riotously while water gushed out of the wall.

"Can you take care of this, Younger Brother?" Jeanie asked me innocently as she headed back down to the party. I nodded and proceeded to do the best drunken plumbing a twenty-one-year-old Midwestern boy knew how to do. Then I went out into the street and ran headfirst into the side of a parked car to relieve a little stress.

It was the early sixties and I was living in a part of Los Angeles called Laurel Canyon with a couple of older gals named Jen and Jeanie. People were beginning to live together in a communal fashion as "brothers and sisters," and Jen and Jeanie treated me as if I were their kid brother and they were my older sisters.

I had met my "older sisters" some months before at a favorite hangout, Barney's Beanery, a ramshackle Santa Monica Boulevard restaurant that had been drawing high- and lowlife clientele for several decades. They both were still in their thirties and they were legends of sorts. Together, the two generated a bright light, a kind of aura that all sorts of people were drawn toward. They took a quick look at me and called me "Younger Brother," a role I took on wholeheartedly, and crashing at their bungalow in lower Laurel Canyon was wonderful—until it wasn't. The household was a cultural hub of artists. There was a constant stream of amazing people coming and going, and I found myself in an exotic world that I didn't fully understand and began to wish I could be part of.

Although I was never invited to sleep with either of them, both women were very liberal with their romantic alliances. The man who had broken the sink was the gregarious but deeply troubled painter John Altoon.

Altoon was an abstract painter and a big deal in the L.A. art world. Tragically, John is as well-known for the art he destroyed, always his own, as he is for what he created. Either his perfectionist sensibility was incapable of satisfaction, or he became convinced that his art was inadvertently revealing characteristics that he'd rather have kept private. Now I can relate, but back then, I had no idea what to make of it.

In addition to Altoon's regular visits, actor Lawrence Tierney lived at the house for a while as well, and lots of wild characters used it as a crash pad. Jeanie and Monty Budwig, bass player at the venerable Hollywood jazz club Shelly's Manne-Hole, were an item, and every kind of musician, artist, actor, and party person rolled in and out of our pad at all hours.

Jen and Jeanie decided who was welcome and who had to be shown the door, and I became their unofficial bouncer, sending dozens of wannabes and troublemakers back down to the city if they weren't welcome. Over the course of my months at the house, every time either gal said a quick word or signaled to me with her eyes, the misbehaving son of a bitch was toast.

One of the perks of my position was that people who visited the house were eager to stay on my good side and quick to offer me every mood-altering tablet or pill I could consume. Uppers, downers, twice-arounders, Jeanie would inspect each and inform me which I could keep and which required a pilot far more experienced than me.

Damn, that house was always happening! One night, the R&B band the Treniers were so stoned they couldn't talk but could play jump blues for hours on end; then the next evening the walls of the house were covered with paintings for an impromptu art show. You never knew what the night would hold except that it would be unconventional and that everyone would be full-tilt boogie.

It was the coolest scene I'd ever been part of and Jeanie in particular was a fascinatingly liberated woman—someone living far before her time in many ways. Though the house was the hippest, most creative place in West L.A., I was on the verge of dying. Around-the-clock booze and pills were beginning to take their toll on my soul. And if one more heroin addict needed to be dumped in downtown L.A., I might've joined him.

Chapter 2
A Date with Humble Pie

How did I get here? A Midwestern boy about to career off the tracks?

It was 1962. I'd made my way to Los Angeles and Pasadena City College, playing football in my third junior college in as many years as coaches were delighted when an athlete of my caliber walked on. But I didn't last at any of the colleges because I never intended to go to class—and succeeded in that brilliantly.

I had inherited my mother's nonconformity and propensity for imaginative living. Schools, churches, institutions of every kind were bullshit as far as she was concerned—and she taught me well, worried that school might otherwise turn me into a robot.

I knew I didn't want anyone telling me what I was going to be, and I craved every kind of experience I could get. I didn't envision myself as a student—or anything else but an athlete. As far as the future was concerned, I felt destiny would eventually take hold, so in the meanwhile I would concentrate on fishing and football and surviving Jen and Jeanie's. I liked Southern California and sure as hell wasn't heading back to the Midwest any time soon.

It was a day like any other when destiny came calling. My good friend Tom Connelly, who was an actor at the Pasadena Playhouse, suggested that I come watch a play in which he was appearing.

Those days I was up for just about anything, so I agreed to go. The play was okay, but I didn't really think about it again until a few weeks later, when Tom asked me to join him for an acting class led by Bryan O'Byrne, who had been a successful character actor for many years and who now coached several young talents. Tom was being considered for a major role in a new television series based on the steamy novel *Peyton Place,* and he knew he had to work as much as possible with Bryan.

Bryan lived near the top of Laurel Canyon, and on the day he ushered us into his house, Tom was scheduled for one-on-one instruction. Tom told him I just wanted to observe; Bryan wouldn't have it. He informed us if I wanted to stay, I'd need to read for him, too. I wasn't really comfortable with the notion, but neither did I want to cause Tom problems, so I reluctantly agreed.

Inside Bryan's house, I simply observed as he worked with Tom for a while, the two of them discussing the family life of the character he was reading, imagining where he would have grown up and what his relationship with his brother would have been like. I had never considered before that an actor had to know more, imagine more, than simply the words the playwright had given him to speak. That I could use my imagination to create an entire life for the character, then slip inside it and try it out.

When they took a break, Bryan offered me something to read and I studied a bit before we reconvened. I can't remember what it was except that it was some famous soliloquy that young male actors cut their teeth on in those days, and when I started to read I was nervous as hell. If I'd been trying out a new sport or meeting a girl or something, I would have been fine. But then I thought, Fuck it, I can read this thing, and I did. Silence followed. It was obvious from the look on their faces that I'd done something right. Bryan finally said, "Well, that was good, Nick."

Later he motioned for me to follow him, and out of Tom's earshot he said, "You don't know it yet, but you're an actor. When *you* realize you are, I'll be happy to work with you. You've got the thing—that someone either has or he doesn't. You've got it."

It felt nice to hear, but I was more certain I still had some football in me. I continued to define myself—to the degree I gave the subject any real thought—as an athlete, and Bryan's encouragement was interesting, yes, but I didn't make too much of it that afternoon. Besides, I had a decent job at the moment.

Jim Nelson, who was a fullback with me at PCC, was a young guy with a persuasive personality who had enthusiastically informed me that the local ironworkers' union was hiring. There was lots of work to be had, he said, because Los Angeles was installing storm drains throughout the city, and big, strong kids like us could quickly learn to haul pipe and hand rebar to the fellows who tied it. It would be hard but satisfying, and the best part, Jim contended, was that we could work for three months at fourteen dollars an hour—a fortune in those days—then draw unemployment and find other adventures for the rest of the year.

President Kennedy was still in the White House. The decade was beginning to rev up. The established order of conventionality was teetering and verging on its collapse, and you could feel the terrible stranglehold on every free thought—the demand for conformity that had driven me mad in my early years in Iowa and Nebraska—beginning to loosen. Change was in the air, but none of us had a clue where we or the times were going. All that was clear to me was that having a bit of money in my pocket and a few good fellows to travel from one bar to the next with was enough. Yet as my interests began to widen, I started to feel that I was growing out of my old skin, and I was quickly going to need a new set of skills if I was to survive it. L.A. teemed with cultured creativity, and I felt like a rube in its midst. My old persona had evolved under the cultural regime of the conformity-loving forties and fifties, and was patently unsuited for whatever lay ahead.

Jim Nelson fit into the new vibe of the sixties seamlessly and could shuck and jive with the best of them. As did the leader of my union local, 433, an H. L. Mencken aficionado named Conrad Monte. A cynical son of a bitch, Conrad hated everyone and everything and was always eager to tell anyone who would listen why. I didn't like Conrad, but it sounded to my young ears like he'd read every book ever written.

It was Conrad who unknowingly spurred my desire to begin educating myself a bit about why the world wags and who wags it, and, like he did, I began to spend lots of my free time in bookstores—a new pastime for me.

It was in a Hollywood bookstore, too, where I smoked my first joint. I knew the store's owner from Barney's Beanery. The bookstore was nearby and all of us who frequented Barney's acted as if we were fast friends, and the bookstore owner, whose name I can't remember, invited me into his stockroom, where he casually lit up.

A few puffs later, I knew weed and I were going to go steady for a while. I felt both calmer and more clearheaded, and began to think about things in intriguing ways. I noticed that I was at ease with myself—at peace with the person who often made me so uncomfortable—in ways I never otherwise was, except perhaps on the football field.

I loved it. My mind seemed to kick into a higher gear. I connected disparate dots as it encouraged my already fertile imagination, and I remember going back to the bookstore a day later and buying an ounce—which we called a lid—from the store's proprietor. I took it "home, locked myself in my bedroom, and stayed stoned for most of a week, getting to know myself in entirely new ways and pondering just who was growing out of this new skin of mine.

I didn't have any answers yet, but I was getting better at framing the questions. I knew I liked the vigorous work of punking steel—a chore that involved lugging giant pipes from trucks to huge holes in the ground. I liked having some money to spend on each evening's entertainment, and I liked Barney's and the carnival of people it attracted. The story was that Errol Flynn, Clark Gable, Rita Hayworth, Judy Garland, and many others all had been regulars in their day. I didn't know about that, but an array of characters was always in-house in the early 1960s, including art-world up-and-comers like painter Ed Ruscha; photographer, painter, and actor Dennis Hopper; and character actor Lawrence Tierney.

I was barely twenty-one and strong as an ox, and I'd already become very well acquainted with alcohol before my arrival in Southern California. I loved adding other kinds of inebriates to my recreational repertoire and exploring where they would take me, but even I struggled to hold my own with the over-the-top kinds of insanity that were standard fare at Jen and Jeanie's. I knew my tenure there likely would be brief.

It was at about that time when a Rolls-Royce slowed to a stop one day as my buddies and I were punking steel at the intersection of Beverly Glen and Sunset

Boulevard. A well-dressed, chinless man rolled down the car's window, caught my attention, and asked, "Are you an actor?" I told him I wasn't, and that seemed to be the answer he was hoping for.

If I wanted to be one, he informed me, he could help; he promised to put me in the movies because he was a Hollywood agent. What he didn't explain was that his name was Henry Willson, or that he had paved the way for Robert Moseley to become Guy Madison, for Arthur Kelm to morph into Tab Hunter, or for an awkward truck driver named Roy Scherer to turn into Rock Hudson.

Bryan O'Byrne's recent revelation to me that I had what it took to be an actor still was simply that—a bit of encouragement I couldn't turn into either cash or a career—but neither did the idea seem like a terrible one. So, when Willson continued his introduction by handing me his card with his home address scribbled on the back and inviting me to come to dinner that night to discuss possibilities for stardom, I couldn't refuse.

Willson answered the door at his Bel Air home a few hours later and the two of us had drinks and dinner, and yes, he was absolutely certain that I could be a big star—if it was something I truly wanted. When I agreed that the prospect intrigued me, he excused himself for a moment and returned wearing only a silk dressing gown.

"Hello, cuddle bunny!" he said, and suddenly I understood.

A feeling of deep unease shot through me from head to toe; I awkwardly excused myself and was quickly out the door, thinking that Hollywood could wait. I was outta there.

It wasn't until much later that I learned that most of the would-be actors Willson represented were homosexual, bisexual, or simply cooperative with him in order to get gigs. My early departure from his home that evening ensured, of course, that Willson would not become my agent and that my movie star days were a long way away—if they were ever to come.

Bryan O'Byrne, it was clear, had no interest whatsoever in creating a similar kind of apprenticeship with me. Bryan was a good man, I soon came to understand, and he was a great acting coach, and his appraisal of my latent talent had been an honest one.

I thought about it regularly as life at Jen and Jeanie's escalated and I struggled to understand and hang with the much older, more sophisticated artist group. There was also chaos. Some mornings the house would be such a god-awful mess that Jeanie would tell me she wanted nothing more than to die, and she meant it, I know. Jeanie struggled with deep depression, something I recognized because I was no stranger to that paralyzing fog in which every element of your being grows afraid and crushingly numb. But as long as I simply chatted with her as she sat in a kitchen chair and watched me dive into a mountain of dishes, her deep anguish would subside and she could imagine living a day or two longer.

One day soon after she had discovered she was pregnant—and did not want to be—she sent me to a Laurel Canyon store where someone would be waiting to give me some special sugar cubes he had prescribed for her. I did as she requested, then discovered that each one contained a heavy hit of LSD. Jeanie planned to consume so much of the drug that she would miscarry, she said. She told me explicitly that I was not to touch or taste the sugar cubes, and I trusted her and let them be.

I don't think the LSD had its desired effect on Jeanie in the end, but the memory persists because I was tied up in knots about whether something terrible might happen to her, taking so much of a drug that I wasn't familiar with yet. Being way out of my element was wearing on me, and together with my old friend anxiety, it created a lurking feeling that my old ways of being were no longer enough to get me to wherever it was I wanted to go next.

I was in danger of washing out of my third junior college in as many years, and numerous injuries were signaling the end of my athletic eligibility and closing the door on my one fail-safe passion. Football had beautifully fed my adrenaline addiction. My adolescent habit of being so jacked up during a game that I would either foam at the mouth or sob uncontrollably continued. My old identity was tightly tethered to the gridiron, and the possibility that football was about to be absent from my life forever was one I hadn't begun to consider until now. And when I allowed myself to truly consider it, I was confused and lost.

What I did in response to the confusion was party at a level that might have killed otherwise healthy horses. Barney Anthony, the owner of Barney's Beanery, literally lifted me out of Santa Monica Boulevard on more than a few occasions when I had passed out and was in danger of being run over. I continued my bizarre tendency to head-butt parked cars. Fortunately, I wasn't one of those kids who is compelled to pick fights; instead I used self-inflicted physical pain to distract me from my emotional state. Something in me recognized that I deeply needed the safety of Bryan O'Byrne's concern and counsel. I needed to get a clearer view of how to begin making a life for myself, but all I really knew was that I was at a loss for how to proceed.

I began to spend lots of time with Bryan, and, thank God, he continued to see an actor somewhere deep inside the man I was struggling to become. He encouraged me to focus on acting as a method of studying the human soul. "Where did that thought come from?" he would ask of the character I was reading. "Why does he feel the way he does?"

Bryan's own acting philosophy centered on scene study and repetition in the manner of the legendary Sanford Meisner, who taught aspiring actors about the essential "reality of doing." Meisner and Bryan believed that repetition in acting, like prayer, bores your ego into complacency, a trick that lowers an actor's guard and enables him to bare himself in front of an audience—or the whole of the universe. This, I feel, is why the most vulnerable among us often make the finest actors, and why saints get mistaken for fools. But humility doesn't guarantee success or revelation, only the possibility.

With repetition and the conquering of ego, Bryan was convinced, an actor can become open to pain, humiliation, and degradation—all risks that you must open yourself to in the performing arts. I remember loving the idea that actors—and everyone—can learn how to construct grace in the face of the daily grind. Perhaps acting could help this washed-up football player, half-assed ironworker, and already-well-on-his-way young addict handle life.

I began spending as much time in Bryan's orbit as I could, crashing nights on his couch at the top of the canyon instead of farther down the hill among the wild revelries at Jen and Jeanie's. Then one day Bryan offered me a bed and I gratefully said yes, knowing that I was very rapidly unraveling, careening toward a date with humble pie or death. I didn't know it at the time, but my manic energy, mixed with a deep desire to change without the tools of knowing how, had pushed me to the edge. I'd made a young man's mistake of challenging the darkness.

As I think back on it, it's curious that although self-exploration became my obsession during that existential crisis, my acting studies with Bryan apparently didn't have anything to do with performing or forging a career path. All I needed was the permission to feel each feeling and experience every emotion. Contradictory thoughts no longer felt like character flaws; instead they were doors to a series of different rooms in my head, and I wanted to visit them all. Every bit of make-believe, every role I took on in Bryan's book-cluttered living room, seemed to offer me a chance to be reborn.

Thankfully, Bryan saw when I hit a crucial point in my process. He was attuned to studying the psyche as an actor, and my erratic behavior of passing out in public and running my head into cars was signaling to him I needed help. He could see that I needed my own space to allow the full breakthrough/breakdown. Once more he came to my rescue and dialed up my parents, who were living in Phoenix.

"Nick needs your help," Bryan explained. "You should come get him." Their only son was cracking up—that's what Bryan conveyed—and they took the telephone call for the weighty notice it was, because my dad showed up the next day, tossed me and a few possessions in his car, and drove us back to Phoenix. I don't remember his saying a single word as the sedan rolled across the desert, and it would be a long and consequential decade before I danced with Los Angeles again.

Chapter 3
Zero Point

The silence that had consumed the car continued when we reached my parents' house in Arizona. My mother seemed to inherently understand my need for space and didn't require explanations any more than my father had, and my maternal grandmother, who had begun to live with them, was simply happy to see me and told me what a good-looking boy I'd become. But I sure as hell didn't look good; I was a husk of the young man I'd been the last time she had seen me. I slunk into a bedroom my mother had prepared for me and closed the door, determined to be in solitary confinement for a long while.

My memories of that time remain surprisingly vivid, perhaps because there has been no other stretch like it in my life, and perhaps, too, because I still carry those feelings with me. There was the fear-fueled anxiety that whirled on a debilitating loop inside my brain. Then panic would come slithering under the bedroom door like a vapor, taking my breath away as it consumed me and strapping me to the bed as if I were tied to it with ropes.

When I tried to escape by burying myself beneath the sheets, suffocating hallucinations overtook me, including a recurrent one that I was drowning in a sea of shit that smelled so awful it induced real projectile vomiting. It was harrowing, and it was grisly. Only occasionally would I get a few minutes of relief before I grew panicked once more by the certainty that I would drown, and I had to accept the awful fate that I would die in shit. My efforts to hog-tie my fear, to wrestle it and control it and will it away, backfired. I could control absolutely nothing, and when I tried I'd simply find myself flushed down that hellish toilet all over again.

My room became a self-imposed sanitarium. I held the key and no one confined me to the cell except me, yet I virtually never left. My mother would leave food trays outside the door that sometimes I nibbled from, and it was only in the middle of the night that I would give myself permission to leave, creeping down the hall to the kitchen in search of a glass of juice. Occasionally,

I'd find my grandmother in the kitchen, awake and in a rush to begin her day. She was what my mother called "charmingly vague," which is a nice way to say suffering from dementia.

"Matthew, I'm late for work!" She spoke to me as if I were her long-dead husband. I would take on my grandfather's countenance and demeanor as best I could and gently escort her back to her room to settle into bed again. It was strangely soothing to pretend to be someone I was not.

Almost a lifetime later, I recognize that often the best remedy for my own problems is to offer someone else a helping hand. Sadly, I haven't always remembered this trick, but it was the one way in which I connected with another human being during those many months, and I adored my grandmother.

I began to jot down my thoughts and experiences, making a record of the zero point at which I found myself. I included a tortured self-appraisal or two. "I'm a petty lunkhead, unskilled, and socially awkward," I scribbled. This was true, and recognizing that was something of a breakthrough, although it certainly didn't feel like it at the moment. Reviewing the notes produced another conclusion: I read at a sixth-grade level because of dyslexia. That year I proceeded to put my efforts into learning how to deal with the way my eyes tracked letters on the page—right to left in columns, like the Chinese system—even working with a tutor briefly that year to help me improve.

Then joyfully I read, and reread, the bundle of acting books and plays I had purchased a few months before at the Samuel French bookstore on Sunset, as well as those I had "borrowed" from Bryan.

I devoured Richard Boleslavsky's *Acting: The First Six Lessons,* plays by Anton Chekhov, and my self-help bible—Konstantin Stanislavski's *An Actor Prepares. An Actor Prepares* is a monumental work that's the diary of a fictional student named Kostya during his first year of training in Stanislavski's hugely renowned "Method" acting system. The Method system is a means of both mastering the craft of acting and stimulating an actor's individual imagination and creativity.

I found out that Stanislavski's ideas had initiated a revolution in the theater and the ways in which actors approached their roles, but what mattered most among my budding epiphanies in that Phoenix bedroom was the notion—not unique to Stanislavski—that we're all actors, onstage or off, a simple idea that slowly began to quiet my self-loathing and allow me to be many contradictory things at once.

My parents were likely scared to death, yet they never showed it, offering me comfort and privacy throughout my ordeal as they held their counsel and simply hoped for the best. I took it for granted, not realizing at the time that I had won the parental lottery. I might have had a very different kind of experience with different parents.

Electric-shock therapy was in vogue during that era, considered a cure-all by many psychiatrists and general practitioners and prescribed for non-ailments like homosexuality and hyperactivity, often wrecking otherwise promising lives. Had my mom and dad taken me to the doctor, who the hell knows what he might have prescribed or whether I might have been brain-shocked or even lobotomized as a way to make me "normal" again?

Luckily, "normal" was a word my parents never applied to me, whether I was in the midst of a crackup or not. They treated me with remarkable patience, then acceptance, over the course of my many months in their house, and I was about to reward them with dramatic ingratitude, I'm sorry to say. Once I learned they were of my mind's own anxious creation, I grew less terrified of the dreams. The only real result of that improvement was a willingness to venture outside my bedroom a bit more and wander around the house in the wee hours of the morning.

On one foray out into the darkened house, I came

across a reel-to-reel tape recorder and moved it to my room. I began to record hours of monologue focused on my growing up in Iowa and Nebraska. For hours on end, I raged about every conceivable slight or wound I had received from birth until graduation from high school, and I leveled the worst of the blame for my problems at Mom and Dad. They were responsible, I tearfully told the tape recorder, for stunting my growth, inflicting terrible emotional damage, and boxing me in so thoroughly that I had no notion of how to interact with the world I encountered. I told them as a baby I had absorbed the war fears of their generation. That deep, repressed societal fear and consequent conservatism was another thing I had to push through and let go of while I was locked in my room.

I was sure they were the reason my childhood had been so traumatic; they were culpable for sending me off to college unprepared; they were largely responsible for my crack-up.

As I held the machine's little microphone close to my lips and spewed out my pent-up fury, I imagined playing the tape for them and watching as they uneasily squirmed. They would finally have to confront their failings as parents—and I would be free to start my new life unencumbered.

Aside from the delusional-brat routine, I was standing in the face of fear and accepting my glitches. Now I can see how selfish it was to blame it all on my parents, but at the time, my ranting monologue was part of a new awareness and self-analysis. It was clear mine was never going to be a linear evolution, but the next steps to growth were making themselves clearer. Scrubbed of my old identity and fortified with sage new teachings from my beloved books, I was finally ready to explore my career ambitions. Acting it was: a vocation, a survival tool, and a destiny all rolled into one.

Chapter 4
Corn-fed

The earliest story I remember was told through the lens of my father and mother. Who isn't formed by the successes and losses of the generation before them? My dad's name was Franklin Arthur Nolte, but because of his height, everyone called him Lank. He was a farmer's son who almost dropped out of high school, then received an engineering degree and lettered in football three years in a row at Iowa State beginning in 1929. He was a whopping six feet six inches tall and weighed two hundred sixty pounds when he played ball—at a time when men in America just didn't get that big. The fact that everyone turned to stare at Dad when we entered a room made a serious impression on me. He was always conscious of his stature and compensated with an easygoing, calm nature. People called his brothers Poob and Beaner; they were gigantic, too, and the Nolte brothers were known for their gentle spirits as much as for their size.

Yet Dad didn't seem easygoing so much as simply a shell of a man the first time I remember meeting him. I had been born shortly before he was shipped out to fight in World War II, and I must have been about four or so when my older sister, Nancy, and I were told someone special was about to arrive, and our house in Ames, Iowa, buzzed with anticipation that day. Our mother was all dressed up and everyone in our extended family waited eagerly in the living room. But then the front door opened and a skeleton walked in.

Dad had spent the past four years fighting the Japanese in the South Pacific, and the terror of war and the relentlessness of malaria had reduced him to a sack of bones. He had lost at least a hundred pounds since he had said goodbye to us, my mother later explained, and although she didn't tell us much more, she did want us to know that now he was quite different from the robust and handsome guy who had kissed us before leaving several years before.

The war took a great toll on my dad. Nancy and I would steal into his bedroom as he napped, staring at him and trying to make what we could of this man we were told we now should love. I wouldn't understand until much later that damaged soldiers like my dad had kept our country from falling to tyranny, yes, but their sacrifices deeply affected American culture as well in the late 1940s and 1950s.

They had witnessed in profoundly personal ways the horror of what humankind was capable of, and it scared the hell out of them. They lost faith in man's basic decency, and they clung to rules and conformity as the best ways to survive—something they had learned well as soldiers. I observed this need for structure and orthodoxy in my dad, my coaches, and authorities of every kind while I was growing up. They were men who had become desperate to repress their emotions, and they became callous, uncommunicative, and rigid. The suffocating tone of 1950s America was something for which they were in large part responsible—but for which it was very difficult to fault them. Dad wanted no more fighting. He wanted quiet and he wanted peace, and when I looked at him I knew I sure as hell never wanted to be in a war.

Graduating from Iowa State University with a degree as an engineer, Dad was enough of an athlete, too, that he might have been able to play professional football. But the war had interrupted his life—and our lives with his—in very dramatic ways. Because my father had an engineering degree, they had recruited him into the army where he earned a bronze star as a major. He and my mother had met, courted, married, and made babies fueled by an early energy and passion, but the war sapped my father's zest for seizing life, and he chose to spend his entire postwar career traveling the Midwest selling big irrigation pumps for a company called Fairbanks Morse.

If the war muted Dad's spirit, it emboldened my mother's. Like many wives left at home in 1942, she had gone to work while her husband fought overseas, and she had absolutely no interest in returning to homemaking when the war finally ended. She was genuinely glad to have her husband home, we knew, yet her anger lingered a long time over his decision to leave the military.

Mother had enjoyed quite a bit of autonomy while Dad was in the war and she was eager to continue carving out as much liberty as she could in her life. Yet Dad did not want the constant mobility that staying in the service would have demanded, and he had lost whatever career drive he once had had—something with which Mom's ambition was in a constant state of tension over the years.

Helen King Nolte also had a problematic relationship with her parents and her sister. My grandparents were engineering professors at Iowa State, and Mom's older sister, Harriet, with whom she was competitive throughout her life, taught at the University of Oregon. Because she had grown up surrounded by educators whom she called "snobs," Mom developed a rebellious disregard for teachers at every level of education. They were people who couldn't make it in the real world, she hammered into the heads of both Nancy and me. Imagination could teach you far more than you could learn in any classroom. Imagination was the only crop worth cultivating, she said.

Despite her lifelong contempt for what Midwesterners labeled "book learning," my mother earned a degree from Iowa State before heading to Chicago in her twenties. Mom had striking blond hair and the kind of face and figure that many would call a "knockout," and she worked as a model in newspaper print ads before she took a job at the city's renowned department store, Marshall Field's. There she developed an interest in retail fashion that would grow into a long career that she loved. While there she was asked out by a member of the Capone family. My parents had met and dated at Iowa State, but had gone their separate ways. When my father found out she was dating a Capone, he immediately drove to Chicago to propose. Man, that would have been a whole different childhood for me if he hadn't!

Her style, like her personality, was unique and thoughtful. My mother had an eye for clothes and she respected those who could tweak an outfit, making it their own. In her mind, this suggested the adventurous resourcefulness of a lived life. She was always well dressed but never afraid to get her hands dirty. She expertly upholstered our furniture and was a tailor, too, and I grew up knowing how to use a needle and thread and was very handy with a sewing machine. She taught me everything about fabrics, and styles, and although it was difficult to find a way to stand out in that cookie-cutter era, in high school, I managed to do so by wearing my own custom-made shirts with sleeves that were fully six inches longer than normal and flowers I had sewn on the pockets. To this day, I enjoy my own unique style, regardless of what is popular or expected.

In time, Mom became a retail clothing buyer for major department stores in all the towns and cities in which we lived. The male-dominated auction floors of Chicago and New York never intimidated her for a moment. She was supremely confident in her unique sense of style and taste, and would battle anyone who doubted her vision. She held merchandising managers, almost all of whom were men, in contempt. Their lack of interest in the products they sold and their total lack of respect for women galled her, and the fact that she had to do battle with them virtually daily exacted a heavy price.

The rage Mom was forced to stifle at work would boil over at home, often as she cleaned up after dinner and railed aloud about the prejudices against women she experienced. Racial discrimination made her blood boil, too, and she would punctuate her fury by smashing dishes and battering our kitchen appliances, outbursts that would shock Nancy and me and deeply embarrass and irritate our father. When Mom would fly into one of her fits, Dad simply would shepherd Nancy and me safely to our rooms, putting on a brave face.

I don't remember words like "permissive" or "liberal" ever being used in Iowa in those days, but my mother was undoubtedly both. On days when she had trouble rousting me from bed, because I either wasn't feeling well or simply didn't want to go to school, she would offer me a "vitamin." The pills were Dexedrine—in reality speed—and taking one would have me bouncing off the walls in no time, eager as hell to get to school and wreak whatever havoc I could.

Mom prided herself on her absolute honesty, something that would often be hurtful. She'd never really wanted either of us, she told us several times, and that revelation wounded my sister and me. Were we that bad? we wondered. Did she really wish we were never born?

No. She gave us a mountain of motherly love, and her affection and support for us never wavered. All she meant, at last we came to understand and accept, was the truth that she had never longed to have children before we were born. Nancy and I were the products, plain and simple, of the lust she and my father had shared for each other before he went off to war.

More troubling was Mom's regular assertion that she would divorce Dad once the two of us were grown. This was something she was happy to predict in front of him as well as her children, and although my father was silent whenever she repeated her plan, it worried Nancy and me enough that we always met her confident claim by begging her to stop kidding around.

My mother took a Dexedrine tablet of her own every morning before work, and drank two or three vodka tonics each evening. She loved to entertain, and friends, in turn, were always eager to join the parties at the Noltes'. Young or old, when people were at our house they could be themselves, free from expectation or judgment, and she demanded them to be, in fact.

Booze was a vital social lubricant during that era, and I was permitted to drink at home as soon as I turned fifteen.

Women admired Mom's strength of character and her self-determination; men, in turn, admired just about everything about her they could identify. She was great fun and always had an opinion on every topic. People with whom she was close—even my buddies from school—sought her advice on matters large and small, and several remained close to her long after I'd lost touch with them. My ability to tell a decent story also came from my mom, of course.

Nancy was two years older than me, always taller, and the better athlete of the two of us. If she had been born a couple of decades later, she would have been an Olympic swimmer, I'm certain. But women and sports were believed to be an odd combination as she and I were growing up, and virtually no public school programs existed for athletic girls.

However, when we moved to Waterloo, a small Iowa city that wasn't much bigger than Ames but was far more urban, we discovered a fine aquatic center, an excellent swimming program, and a great coach named Dick Malone, under whose tutelage Nancy thrived. The water just seemed to part before her. She never lost a race that I can remember, and I think her competitive swimming days were the happiest of her childhood.

When I was in the second grade, the family left Ames and made our way to Waterloo when Dad accepted a transfer with Fairbanks Morse, and Mom got a position as a buyer for Black's department store, which was a great new opportunity. Our first day in town, Mom marched us from house to house in our new neighborhood, introducing herself and Nancy and me to the housewife who answered each door, explaining that she was a working woman and that because of her busy schedule they could expect to see the two of us regularly playing without a chaperone. Nancy was old enough to look after us both, she said. It was embarrassing for us, but Mom wasn't about to let anyone think for a moment that she was a negligent mother, and it was just like her to speak first to people before she would dare let them make an assumption about her.

Nancy's upbringing was a raw deal for her. Not only was she routinely saddled with the thankless task of looking after me, but our parents were far stricter with her than they were with me. Yet she rose to my defense time and again throughout our childhood, as she simply accepted that her little brother was eccentric at a time when a child who was unconventional was about as welcome as a kid with head lice.

I was lucky that my parents generally tolerated my eccentricities, even accepting without argument my announcement one day that I would no longer be attending church. The only times my mother demanded our best behavior was when she wanted the whole family to attend a graduation or retirement ceremony at the university. She would scrub Nancy and me to a high shine and force us into uncomfortably formal attire, insisting on our best behavior no matter how terribly boring the event happened to be. "Sit up straight, don't fidget, and look everyone in the eye when you shake their hands," she would instruct. Funny that, despite her scorn for education and all its trappings, there were times when it was vitally important for her to demonstrate what a fine mother she was, as well as to show off the couple of obedient and good-looking kids she was raising!

The Iowa woods were paradise. Once or twice a week Mom would take Nancy and me out, and we felt most at home there. We would hunt for mushrooms and splash in the creeks, and although we never got to know him, she made sure to point out the cave where a solitary man lived.

Mom was a nature girl and always had been. I have a photo I love of her that to me sums her up. In it, she's five years old, wearing bib overalls, and with one hand holds her dog by his leash; the other is balled into a fist and planted on her hip. "Take your damn picture so I can get back to exploring!" her expression says, and she carried that same defiant attitude with her throughout her life. Defiant. Freedom meant everything to her— she could admire a man who was free to live in a cave, if he chose to—and she worked hard to face down the fear that people would take her freedom away.

Even when I was young, I understood my mother's fear of being restricted, her dislike of rules. I could tell, too, that other adults shared that fear. Yet most simply shut themselves down and did as they were expected to do. I had soaked that feeling up. That's what I carried. It was trying to get out of me. I found the best way to deal with that was to do outrageous things. That's how I combated fear. Pull a prank. Tell a lie. Or retreat to nature.

I called myself a river kid, because the big rivers on whose banks we lived were my soul mates, in many ways. I could sit under a tree for hours and look out at the moving water and do nothing more than *imagine*. Rivers and their banks were both fun parks and refuges throughout my early years. Society's rules, which really flummoxed me from the get-go, meant nothing out in the wilderness, where it never mattered if your shirttail was tucked in or your hair was combed, and Mother Earth had a wonderful way of punishing arrogance and stupidity. The Skunk, the Cedar, the Iowa, and the Missouri were wide ribbons of water in which I didn't so much observe nature as become part of it—swimming without giving a thought to submerged trees or currents, collecting snakes and other reptiles I kept in jars and boxes in my bedroom, fishing for carp, and feeling wonderfully alive. I imagined myself as a twentieth-century Huckleberry Finn, with a bicycle instead of a raft.

Like my mother, I had my own keen sense of style, and I liked to bleach my jeans until they were virtually white. I remember the time that I waded into the water to retrieve a fat carp I'd caught. But my jeans—their fabric weakened by all the bleaching—ripped apart as I lunged for the fish. So, I had no option but to wrap my shirt around my middle and march downtown to Black's department store—big carp in hand—where I found my mother and announced, "Hey, Mom, I gotta get some pants!" She laughed, full of pride.

Anybody who seemed to disrespect nature, or who failed to be moved by it in some elemental way, risked having me toss them into the river as punishment for their arrogance. But Mom was like me; nature and she were powerfully bonded, and I loved how she encouraged me to embrace everything that was wild and unrestrained.

It was fine with my mom that I was fiery and forceful—I received those traits from her—and I discovered that I possessed a kind of intensity that was both internally and externally powerful. When fear welled up, I'd simply summon a kind of outrageousness that was always inside me. With it, I'd swim the widest stretch of water I could find, mindless of the dangers, or I'd pull a big prank without concern for the trouble in which it might land me.

When I felt that kind of intensity, I also felt free, and I remember that on summer nights I would purposefully go at whatever game we were playing with such abandon that suddenly the entire world would slow down, and I would get dizzy, then nauseous. It was strange—and a little scary—but I never told anyone about it because I was sure they wouldn't understand. I could count on its overtaking me when I let my intensity build to the shouting point. If I pushed just a bit harder, I knew, the world would shift into a *tick, tock, tick, tock,* slow-motion time, and everything would take on a surreal shape.

By the time I was old enough to be playing junior-high football in Waterloo—a game I loved and was really good at—the intensity no longer seemed capable of slowing down time or making me feel sick. Instead,

I often found myself playing with such passion and concentration that I simply started to cry.

I was a punter—I could kick the hell out of the ball—and I also played defensive end, where I was something of a heat-seeking missile when it came to chasing down quarterbacks and sacking them behind the line of scrimmage. I had confidence in my ability to reach the opposing quarterback and drop him before he got off a pass, and part of me wanted to bring that confidence and single-minded passion to every play. Yet football was a team sport, and for the sake of the team I had to remain vigilant in case the quarterback I was chasing suddenly handed the ball to a halfback who would run a reverse to my side of the field, or in case something else unexpected occurred.

I wanted nothing more than to chase down the son of a bitch and drop him like a sack of potatoes. But I had to restrain myself and watch for surprises, too, and the competing demands—my intensity versus my responsibility to protect my side of the field and be ready for whatever happened—were so great they would bring me to tears.

It was odd, and I'm sure it was downright comical at times. My teammates were often completely perplexed—particularly when we were winning by two or three touchdowns and were on our way to *crushing*

the opposing team—about why there were tears running down my face. Friends on the team would come
up to me and lay their arms on my shoulder pads and
suggest, "Man, maybe you should stop playing if it
bothers you so bad. It's just a game, man, it don't
matter that much." And it was impossible for me to
explain, of course. Sure, it was a game, but *that* wasn't
the point. The passion it engendered in me was enormous, and passion felt better than anything else in my
life; I hated to throttle it back in any way. I *craved* big
desire; I wanted it more than I wanted anything else,
and it just happened to be football that lit my passion
like a fire that was virtually impossible to extinguish.

I was a good enough player that I captured a lot of
attention among coaches and scouts and serious fans,
and it looked like I could play high school and college
ball and maybe take my game even further. I was gifted
enough, in fact, that I was invited to attend a summer
football camp run by Bud Wilkinson, the legendary
coach at the University of Oklahoma whose teams were
always national powerhouses.

I would be entering eighth grade that fall and attending with me was my best friend, Charlie Freeman, who
went to a different junior high in Omaha, Nebraska—
where my family now lived—and whom I had met the

year before at a football camp in Minnesota. Wilkinson and his assistant coaches invited twenty Oklahoma kids, who would get special attention because they were homies, and twenty more from nearby Midwestern states. Charlie and I somehow got our dates mixed up and arrived a day early and had nothing to do. We couldn't find a rowboat to ferry ourselves to a girls' camp across the lake, so we had to otherwise occupy our time, and Charlie loved a good prank as much as I did. What could we do to take those boys down a notch?

The Oklahoma boys would be housed in one dorm, with the other half of us in another dorm nearby. We knew the Okies would arrive with some serious attitude, and we wanted to figure out how to humble them from the start. We were struggling to figure out what might work when a brilliant plan suddenly came to me.

To set it in motion, the first thing was for both Charlie and me to take a shit in a single plastic bag—and that was easy enough. Then we sealed it up tight and squished it until it was as big as a plate and no more than a half inch thick. We used a knife to poke it full of little holes, then lifted up one of the mattresses in the Oklahoma dorm, placed our little pancake on the springs, and covered it with the thin canvas that protected the mattress from the springs. I lay down on the bed and Charlie got on his knees to check to be sure nothing was visible from below. Everything was perfect!

After about five days, the Oklahoma boys were complaining constantly about the smell, some suspecting a skunk had died under the floorboards, others certain that their dorm had some sort of plumbing problem. The smell was *horrible* and was getting worse, and, on our day off, the Okies tore their dorm room apart and finally found our little flattened sack of shit. And oh, were they pissed!

A group of them marched immediately up to Charlie and me and said they knew we had arrived early, and knew, too, that we were just the kind of Cornhusker smart-asses to pull a shit prank like that. "I don't know whether to cry or knock the hell out of you," I remember one of them telling me as he poked his fat finger into my chest. Both Charlie and I denied knowing anything about awful smells or a flattened sack of shit or anything of the sort, and Charlie was the kind of guy who exuded strength and success and honesty, so the Okies all *believed* him when he swore he'd had nothing to do with the plot. That left me as their only suspect, and I began to sweat it because they were all mighty angry and somebody—somebody named *me*, it appeared—was going to have to pay.

A couple of days later, I was asleep in my bunk when one of Bud Wilkinson's assistant coaches tiptoed into our darkened dorm and made his way over to my bunk. He sat on the thin mattress beside me, shined a flashlight in my face, and whispered, "You're a son of a bitch, Nolte, and we know you shat in that bag and put it under the bed, and you know what? I'm going to make sure you never play football in any school you go to—anywhere! You might as well give it up now, 'cause your football days are done."

With that, he quietly made his way out of the dorm, and I lay awake in my bunk most of the night and cried because he was an adult, and a coach, and surely his threat was something he could make stick. I wanted to keep playing football more than I wanted to do anything else. Nothing else focused my intensity and gave it meaning and purpose, and I cried because in the long hours before dawn it seemed that I had ended my dream with a stupid, stinking prank.

Chapter 5
Football

Football was my world. There was never a plan B. In high school, it was hard to imagine how anything else might ever seem equally worth my time, hard work, and devotion. So far the poo-poo prank hadn't seemed to affect my high school career, as I had grown bigger and taller, been well coached for the first few years of high school, and by now was a quarterback. I loved running the offense, loved the challenge and responsibility the position demanded, and it seemed certain that I would have a stellar senior year leading the Benson High School Mighty Bunnies on the grid-iron. We were going to be very good, and my final high school football season would lead to many opportunities to play college ball, I was sure.

But then one sweltering day in July as summer practice got under way, I tried to open the locker-room door and found it locked. I banged on it loud enough that head coach Rhees Jeffries finally came to the door and told me I couldn't come in. When I asked why, he said, "Well, the guys are holding a vote on whether you are even going to be asked back on the team." Then he shut the door and locked it again.

When I got home and told my sister, Nancy, she agreed with me that we had to find out what was going on. The whole thing seemed insane. We headed out and found my friend and teammate J. P. Smith, and he was uncomfortable as hell when we approached him.

The coach had pressured everybody on the team to take a vote, he explained, and he'd made it clear that he expected a unanimous show of hands—the coach wanted me gone. "You know, what could we do? What choice did we have?" J. P. said as he turned away, and I was dumbfounded. According to J. P.— who had to know precisely what had occurred in the locker room—I would no longer be the team's starting quarterback, I wouldn't be anyone's backup, wouldn't sit on the bench, wouldn't practice. I was done and that was that, and it was devastating news, far worse than if I'd heard that I had been kicked out of school. School didn't matter; it was *football* that was my education.

Yet before I could ask anything else, J. P.'s defensiveness turned to anger and he added, "You want to fight, motherfucker? I'll fight you."

I said, "No, I don't want to fight, J. P.," and I turned and walked toward our car. But if I was mystified, Nancy, who was home from college for the summer, was *pissed*, and she shouted, "I'll fight you, you motherfucker!"

But I cautioned her, "No, Nancy. You do not want to fight him. I've watched this guy. He's got reach on you, and if you fight him, he'll pick your face apart. You do not want to fight J. P."

"No, *fuck* him!" she insisted. "I'll fight him."

But I managed to get her to back down, and we drove away and went home. The following morning, I got up and was getting ready to head for school when my mom asked where I was going. I told her I wanted to get to school to see what else I could find out. What was the vote about? Why had there been a vote in the first place? What in the hell had I done?

"Okay," Mom said, "but we're moving today. I guess you'll have to figure out where to find us and catch up with us."

"Moving? Where are we moving to?" This didn't make any sense at all.

"We're moving to Westside. Out to West Omaha."

Then she added, as if all kinds of things had been in the works since the afternoon before, "You'll be ineligible for two games and then you'll be eligible for the final eight."

What she meant, I instantly understood, was that I'd be ineligible to play on the Westside High School football team for its first two games, but then I'd be on the team. I didn't know how in the world this had all been considered and decided and set in motion overnight, nor how my parents had decided to move only on *my* account, but apparently, they had even found a new house in the hours since the coach had told me I was cooked.

"Well, I guess I should pack," I said, understanding almost nothing but buoyed by the support and my parents' very quick reaction to this bizarre turn of events.

"That's what I'd do," Mom offered, and that was it, and we packed up and went up to Westside.

It was a long time before I found out what had happened at Benson, before I learned the truth that my expulsion from the football team had nothing to do with the kind of quarterback I was and nothing to do with anything I might have done off the field. One of the rumors was that I had dug holes and hid beer before practice and then got caught drinking it during a practice session. In my own mind, I'd wondered whether putting shit on the bed springs at Bud Wilkinson's football camp a few years before had finally caught up with me, but that seemed wildly improbable, and far more unlikely than what I discovered was the simple truth.

Coach Jeffries wanted me off the team because I was a much better player than the backup quarterback, a kid named Joshua Darley. Yet he wanted Josh to be his starter and play every down because he was having a quiet little affair with Josh's mother. The dean of students at Benson was Josh's father, and that worked in the coach's favor, too, never mind the fact that Josh wasn't as big as me or as tall or as much of an athlete as I was.

The whole deal was more than a little incestuous; it was political as hell, and I was the fall guy. I wasn't an important student in the way that Josh Darley was—at least I wasn't important to the *coach* the way Josh was. As soon as he heard the news that I had been voted off the goddamn team, my dad had gone to Coach Jeffries for an explanation. But Dad didn't like the coach's answers to his several questions, and I know the cowardly coach must have claimed that the matter was out of his hands—my *teammates* wanted me off the team, he surely maintained, and what else could he do but support their wishes?

Dad was far bigger than Coach Jeffries, and he could have crushed him, but instead he simply walked out of his office, went to the bank, and borrowed the down payment he and my mother would need for a new house, found an acceptable tract home over in the Westside district that we could just barely afford, and bought it. Problem solved.

That was the kind of man my father was. In addition to being physically imposing, he had a very palpable, quiet strength that often unsettled people. He didn't make threats and virtually never raised his voice, and the only time he ever truly got mad, according to Mom, was at a party at their friends the Maguires', when, without saying a word in warning, he broke the jaw of a man who was flirting with her.

Dad chose *not* to put a big hurt on Coach Jeffries that day, and I wasn't surprised. High school ball in 1950s Nebraska was almost as big as anything could be, and the coaches at big-city schools like Benson were virtual kings. My father must have known this misuse of power wouldn't be questioned by the community, so he and my mother took us to a new one.

Dad had been a football star at Iowa State, and he knew the game extraordinarily well. I'm sure he loved to watch me play; he seldom missed our practices or games, yet he never talked about my technique or offered me tips or reminisced about his own high school days. We played different positions, for one thing—his big size, even while he was still a kid, had almost assured that he would become a lineman, and he was a good one. But more than that, I know he wanted me to learn by doing—by *playing* the game—and he didn't want me to be burdened with trying to live up to his past accomplishments or his hopes for my own.

He wanted me to learn for myself that football is about solving sudden dilemmas, about learning how and when to react, about choosing in only a millisecond the best option among many dozens. Even though I was much more like my mother than him in most ways, I think we both knew in those days that we shared a passion for the way in which football requires body and mind in equal measure, a passion for the way in which it demands *passion*.

Westside High was a fantastic change. Miraculously the coaches, my teammates, and my fellow students found it easier to accept me as I was than people in Benson had. I was the new kid in school, of course, but I thrived. I remained disinterested in classes, but that didn't get in my way; I was a standout on a very good Warriors football team, and during that final year of high school, I fell in love for the first time, too.

Kathleen Carney was a dark-haired Irish beauty, the best athlete and cheerleader among all the girls in the school. She was also—I was aware from the start—someone who had pledged herself to her boyfriend Bill, who was a year older and away in Lincoln attending the University of Nebraska. Their understanding was that she could date other guys during her senior year, but as soon as she graduated, she would be off to NU herself, where they would be reunited.

Kathy and I began to get close when she offered to help me with my homework and I accepted—although I don't remember ever doing a lick of homework! I was too entranced by her. She liked me, too, and we spent all the time together we could. Soon, we were dating, and before long we had fallen in love. People belittle those first big romantic experiences, but your first love is your biggest love because it's all-consuming, so new and powerful, and for me, falling in love with Kathy had a kind of intensity that someone who craved intensity was certain to find irresistible. My memories of Kathy and how I felt about her—how I felt so wonderfully alive when I was with her—remain fresh in my mind and in my heart. Still fresh in memory, too, was a moment in the springtime when we were driving along in my '55 Plymouth convertible and I swear there were singing angels around, floating. I couldn't see the road at all. It was unbelievable.

Rebel Without a Cause had come out a couple of years before; every teenager in America had seen it two or three times, and even a "good girl" like Kathy was pretty taken with James Dean and the character he played in the film, Jim Stark, a kid who rages against authority as he struggles to understand who he is. Kathy surely saw a parallel or two between Jim and me. "You should become an actor," I remember her telling me as we sat in my convertible, her big dark eyes shining in the low light.

"No," I quickly responded. "I'd never want to be an actor. I couldn't do that. I don't think it's the kind of world a man would want to be in." It was a short conversation, and Kathy didn't suggest it again. It was the first time anyone had ever suggested such a thing. Soon our senior year drew near its close and one night she told me she loved me, she did, but she loved Bill, too, and she had promised to be true to him. She was going back to Bill, but she wanted us to be friends.

I was devastated. I was completely destroyed and was certain my life had just ended. I didn't go sit for my graduation portrait, didn't attend the ceremony, and I remember lying on the grass in Kathy's front yard at about nine o'clock one early summer night, crying my eyes out because I hurt so bad. Kathy never came out to comfort me, but when the front door finally opened, her father stepped onto the porch and said, "Young man, don't you think that's about enough?"

I supposed he was right, and I struggled to my feet and got into the Plymouth and popped the clutch and drove off with the loud squeal of the convertible's tires. I was still crying, and knocking back a quart of beer I had with me to try to get calm, but I was driving erratically and a cop pulled me over. Getting my ass thrown in jail was going to be a fitting end to my misery, I thought, but when the cop asked what the trouble was, I told him, and he genuinely seemed sympathetic to my troubles. When a second police car stopped, the officer explained to his curious fellow cop that this poor kid had a broken heart. It was as simple as that, and both policemen really seemed to care. They were amazing.

"Let's get you home. You need some sleep," one of them said with emotion in his voice. So, they did—one officer driving my Plymouth and the other escorting us in his cruiser. I went to bed as they suggested, although I'm not sure I slept a bit that night—the pain was just too sharp. By morning I knew I had to get as far away as I could from Kathy Carney and Omaha, Nebraska, and all the hurt the world could offer.

When my dad asked me sometime later what I planned to do with myself, I told him I thought I'd try to find a place to play football somewhere. In those days, the timing on finding one's way to college was more fluid. By the time the summer was well under way, Dad and Mom had started making calls to people they knew and eventually we got a yes from Arizona State. Possibly because of my parents' connections combined with my high school record, they were willing to let me "walk on," which meant that although I wasn't recruited, I could try out, and could make the team if I was good enough. The school was a long way from Omaha, so it sounded fine to me, and I packed a few belongings into my little MG convertible, which I'd acquired over the summer as a replacement for the Plymouth, and headed southwest.

I was told on the first day by an assistant coach that my grades weren't high enough to get in as a freshman. I had to go up to a junior college and the coach was expecting me and they had it all arranged. Eastern Arizona College, in the hamlet of Thatcher, is in the southeastern part of the state near the New Mexico border.

Thatcher, I soon discovered, was a town that was heavily Mormon; Safford, its pint-sized twin city about a mile away, was filled with Jack Mormons—people raised in the church who couldn't be bothered to live by its rules and regulations—which meant that the prevailing attitudes in that particular corner of the Wild West were certainly conventional and very conservative. Anything out of the ordinary, like a little English sports car, for example, received immediate and suspicious attention.

The football coach at Eastern Arizona, whose name was Beaks, as I recall, seemed happy to have me come to town. He had arranged a room for me in a dorm at the college. I was punting and playing defensive end in practice, and although there was precious little to like about the place, well, it was football, and when I was on the field my broken heart didn't hurt quite as much as it had a couple of months before.

Then Coach Beaks called me over one day and said, "Nick, looks like we've got us problem. Seems like some folks think you're driving that little car of yours a little too wild-like around town. Around here, you can get yourself arrested with something called a citizen's report, and I guess that's what they got." The coach went on to explain that he had to drive me over to speak with the local judge about my transgressions.

I said okay and the next thing I knew we were parked in front of a little tract house where a gray-haired lady answered the door. She invited us in and the coach and I sat on her couch, and it wasn't until she called me "Mr. Nolte" that I realized she must be the judge.

"Mr. Nolte, I want you to understand that you're driving that little sports car of yours too fast for this town. You are going around turns and spinning your wheels and screeching and it is just too reckless." I nodded and she continued. "We want you to have a good season, but we don't want you to be driving that car around here." I nodded again before she gave me her sentence. "I've made an arrangement with the Safford jail for you to spend thirty nights there. Coach Beaks will pick you up and bring you to Thatcher for your classes and your football practice and he'll take you back to Safford at the end of each afternoon."

When it was my turn to speak, I told the judge that I wasn't too excited about her plan, and she stiffened and told me I really didn't have any choice. Either I would do as she had arranged or I would spend sixty days in jail, which would end any football plans I might have had. I told the judge that, in that case, I would accept her proposal, and she smiled thinly and told me she was glad to hear me say something intelligent, and that was that.

So, the coach drove me over to the imposing old courthouse building in nearby Safford, and inside he introduced me to a desk sergeant who stuck out his hand and said, "Good to meet you, Nick Nolte. You're going to be spending nights with us, I understand." I told him yes, that was the way I understood things, too. He explained that there were normally two or three cells open right behind his desk, and I could choose the one I wanted to sleep in.

I nodded my head in acquiescence and started toward one of the cells before he stopped me. "But you know something, Nick, you don't have to go in there now. You only have to sleep there; you don't have to go in there 'til you get tired."

I told him I didn't know Safford at all, or Thatcher for that matter, and wasn't sure what I'd do when I wasn't sleeping. The friendly police sergeant thought for a moment, then said, "Well, you could ride around with us, I suppose."

A grin must have curled onto my face when I said I'd love to ride around in a police car with him and his fellow officers, and that's exactly what happened. For the rest of my "sentence," I slept in the tiny Safford jail, showered in the locker room at the football field in Thatcher, then spent the rest of my time with the local cops. It was unbelievable.

Over the weeks and months that followed, I got to know where the local gambling games were dependably unfolding, where the well-hidden whorehouses were, where the one or two tough characters in town were likely to be wasting their time. I liked the cops and they liked me, and although I slept with my Westside High senior yearbook every night so I could look at Kathy's photograph as often as I wanted to, the days and nights passed quickly, and little by little, my heart began to mend.

When I finally got to leave the Safford jail at the end of the semester, I moved to a little place my friend and fellow Eastern Arizona teammate Neil Layton offered me, one he cautioned that I'd have to share with his friend Memo, who was a Mexican/Apache, about ten years older than me—and a great guy. Memo soon became a mentor/father figure to me, introducing me to the subtleties of poker and sleight of hand. During that time, I made regular explorations south to the conjoined towns of Douglas and Agua Prieta, the latter a little city on the Mexican side of the border.

There was a particular cantina where I liked to eat, drink tequila, and listen to mariachis play, and nearby was a whorehouse I started visiting. I always found the whorehouses the safest place to be. There I could overcome all the sexual inhibitions that the adults tried to lay up on my generation. It was not free love or anything like that. I was looking for something other than just getting laid; I wanted a sexual education.

That's when I fell for a pretty, pregnant girl. She was dark and exotic and I quickly seemed very special to her. She convinced me to stay for a while and I lasted in Agua Prieta for a month or so on summer break before my money ran out and I knew I had to be going. I still remember—as if it were a scene from a movie—that sweet sloe-eyed girl standing on a low hill, wearing only a thin white slip, crying as I drove away. Something stuck in my throat as I waved into the rearview mirror and crossed the border back into the United States and a return to real life, and I remember thinking that it was a scene I should have played out with Kathy in Omaha if the world had made any sense.

There was a Mormon girl back in Safford, too, who thought I belonged in her future. I wasn't necessarily opposed to the idea, but Coach Beaks was. He was wise enough to know that the two of us were oil and water, and he let me know I was not invited back for another season and made the successful case to me that I ought to head home to Nebraska. I figured I would find my way in due time to another college—just taking enough classes to be eligible to play before

I was kicked out for never attending any—but wasn't in a huge hurry. My teammates sent me off with a pillowcase full of beer.

I had no idea what I'd do once I returned to the Midwest and my parents didn't push, but I needed some kind of work—or income, at least—and I fell into selling fake draft cards to underage kids who wanted to use them to buy booze and get into bars. Back in those days, draft cards didn't include photographs and they weren't laminated or plastic—just a stiff piece of paper on which I could type a name and birth date, then add a counterfeit stamp.

It was crazy, yes, but it paid awfully well. From a contact in Lincoln, I could buy a packet containing a blank draft card, birth certificate, and driver's license for five dollars. It was the draft card that was prized but I was happy to counterfeit all of them, and I would take orders at fraternity houses and hamburger stands and diners, wherever I could find fellas younger than twenty-one who were eager for alcohol, selling them for anywhere from twenty-five to fifty dollars a packet.

The money rolled in for a year and a half or more, and I took on a kind of criminal style, driving an old black funeral limousine, bleaching my hair white, and exclusively wearing black jeans and a black shirt and trench coat. I looked weird, but for some reason no one seemed too concerned with my nonconformity nor my livelihood.

But then one night when I was feeling particularly festive, I rolled my limousine off a hill and it landed right on the green of the ninth hole at the local country club. Scattered across the green were more than a thousand blank IDs—each one with the very same serial number—and it was the fact that the old limo was registered to me that led the FBI to find me a few days later and begin to ask some questions. Could I identify the guy in Lincoln who sold me the cards? *No.* Did I know who Chairman Mao was? *No.* And what was my opinion of the conflict in Vietnam that had begun to make the news? *Huh?*

I had barely heard of Vietnam in the spring of 1961, didn't know the first thing about communism or any other -ism, for that matter, and when those FBI agents started talking to me about the conspiracy in which I was involved, I didn't know what in the hell to make of anything they said. And they, in turn, must have felt that I was the worst master criminal they'd seen.

The word "arrest" hadn't been spoken yet, but my parents were starting to receive telephone calls from well-meaning friends warning them that Nick could be in some serious trouble. My dad didn't seem too concerned because very little truly bothered him, as I've explained, but my mother really freaked out. One day she announced that we had to leave immediately for Uncle Cole's farm in Redfield, Iowa.

"Did he die?" I asked.

"No," she explained, "but it's just time for us to go and get you someplace where people won't find you." So, off we went, and it was a long time before I realized that Mom thought the best thing for us in the face of that trouble was to go on the lam. It's funny to think of now, but it was far from humorous then. Once we were at Uncle Cole's it was decided we would return and face the consequences. It took almost a year, but I was arrested and charged with seven counts of selling counterfeit state and federal documents. I was twenty years old.

The FBI still believed my mission had been to keep my contemporaries out of the army and far from Vietnam—a mission the judge at my sentencing referred to and called by the name *treason*. Yet it *wasn't* a political act of defiance. As far as Vietnam was concerned, I had zero interest in going or fighting anyone there—but I had sold cards so that frat boys could buy beer and whiskey. I merely wanted to make some good money. My goals were no greater than that.

The judge listened to me, then sentenced me to a

$75,000 fine and *seventy-five years* in jail. When I heard him, I suddenly couldn't breathe, couldn't think other than to be sure this was some kind of nightmare, and I almost didn't hear when the judge continued, explaining that he was also going to suspend my sentence, and that under the terms of the Youth Corrections Act, I would be on probation throughout the length of the Vietnam War, but he wanted me to understand, too, that if I got into *any* further trouble, I would be jailed for a very long time to come.

I'm sure that a few of my parents' friends must have believed that I sure as hell should have been sent to prison, that Lank and Helen's boy had turned out to be one of those rebels, but the truth was that I was still trying to make sense of life. I did develop an understanding of what the U.S. was doing in Vietnam, and like so many of my contemporaries, I thought the war was wrong in virtually every way. My sense of racial injustice had been encouraged by my mother since I was very young, as she made sure we always knew African-Americans, so the civil rights movement grew increasingly important to me as well—at least as an idea, as an abstract kind of cause.

Yet I didn't become an antiwar protester or a civil rights activist. Instead, later that year I joined my good friend Garth Peterson, a mysterious and fun guy who had grown up in L.A., in taking a class called Cooking and Food Preparation at the University of Nebraska-Omaha. It was the only class in which we enrolled, and we did so because Garth knew it would be full of girls. It was a great plan, and a successful one, and I fell further under Garth's cool influence when I began to read Jack Kerouac and poets like Corso and Ginsberg and Ferlinghetti, and I started wearing a little fake Beat hat, and Garth and I would go to the black districts in Omaha, where we would listen to jazz and smoke and drink highballs, exploring the rejection of American materialism and opening our minds to spiritual quests and the improvement of the human condition.

But the truth was that I wasn't done with football yet. It wasn't surprising; I'd been an athlete for a couple of decades and a hipster for no more than a year. Football had been the crucible in which I'd ground out my fears, frustrations, and triumphs. I was still young; the game—*playing* the game—still moved me like nothing else could. My parents had relocated to Glendale, California, where my mother had accepted an offer to become a buyer for a prominent department store; my good buddy Chuck Freeman had decamped from Omaha to go make a career for himself in Hollywood, so joining them all in Southern California sounded great. And yes, said the letter from the head football coach at Pasadena City College when he responded to my inquiry, he would be glad to have me walk on to his program as a junior that fall, and together we'd see just what kind of football player I was.

Chapter 6
Little Theatre

In the years since my first heartbreak, I had ventured out of the Midwest and had a brief taste of life. I had slept in a jail cell for a month and a Mexican whorehouse for a month. I'd been convicted of a federal felony and escaped a life of imprisonment by the skin of my teeth. I'd bounced from one junior-college football program to another, then had begun bouncing my head against cars for reasons neither I nor anyone else could explain other than it relieved pent-up stress. Some street-savvy men had taught me how to punk steel and I'd learned a very uncomfortable casting-couch lesson as well. I'd had my eyes opened wide amidst the revelries of the artists of Laurel Canyon, and I'd passed out on the tarmac of Santa Monica Boulevard way too many times, too.

Bryan O'Byrne, almost magically it seemed, had engendered in me an intense interest in acting, then had
called my parents to tell them their son was deeply in
need of a place to reconsider his life. While my contemporaries would have been in their junior years of
college, I had locked myself in a room in my parents'
house in Phoenix, talking to virtually no one except my
senile grandmother. Alone and tormented, I had begun
to read, then reread, every book I could find on the
theory and practice of acting.

Then, at last, I had tape-recorded for my parents a
lengthy indictment of the myriad ways in which *they*
and their generation were responsible for all the confusion and fear that had led to what I had begun to call
my "crack-up." I had blamed them for not teaching
me the skills to deal with my burgeoning new self and
the life outside of sports I now wanted to live. Luckily,
they heard me out and simply shook their heads. They
knew it was a process I needed to do to break away
from my childhood a little and become my own self.
Once that deeply unfair and insensitive little project
was completed, I was ready to leave the four walls in
which I'd confined myself and march out to investigate
the compelling world of acting.

I was full of a vibrant new momentum and my first
stop when I left my parents' house was the Phoenix

Little Theatre, which had been operating since 1920 and was one of the oldest continually operating theaters west of the Mississippi. I was able to wander into the five-hundred-seat venue, which was housed in a mid-century modern complex that included the Phoenix Art Museum, in the middle of the day. The empty stage stood before me like a blank slate in my new life, and I remember making a couple of private promises before walking out into the glaring desert sun again.

As I departed, a man with the unlikely name of Kit Carson encountered me and introduced himself. He didn't seem concerned by my presence, but he eyed me quizzically nonetheless; I was an unlikely visitor. I launched into an overheated explanation of why I was there, but he slowed me down long enough to invite me into his office.

Olan K. Carson was the house director, I quickly learned, a congenial and talented guy who had left Seattle in 1963 to accept an offer to lead the remarkably successful regional theater that was commonly known as the PLT. Once seated in Kit's office, I emptied my guts, telling him everything I could about football and draft cards, the gang at Barney's Beanery and acting lessons in Laurel Canyon, about my newfound reverence for Stanislavski and the year I'd just spent in my bedroom.

Kit listened with interest and more than a little empathy, it seemed, until at last I ran out of gas. Then, just like that, he offered me a role in the company's upcoming production of *The Hasty Heart,* a play by John Patrick. I didn't have to audition, didn't have to prove to him that I had talent; he simply heard something in me, and he must have seen something, too, and he became an important mentor and friend from that first afternoon.

The play was a drama that contained some intentional humor, and it was set in a British military hospital during World War II, but Kit and the PLT had Americanized the story. The character I would play was Digger, an outsider and loner, and I couldn't have imagined a better opportunity for my stage debut, because given my recent past, I certainly didn't have to stretch. I was the second-youngest member of the cast, and I didn't know anyone yet, so playing someone estranged from his companions was easy to pull off, too.

I had read and reread all the acting books. I was totally stoked—my first time onstage, I was going to be acting with a highly respected professional repertory company in a major American city—but about an hour before the curtain came up on opening night, I panicked. Surely, I had *no* business being there! Did I?

I understood that an actor—a *real* actor—must drag himself out there, whatever his baggage, whatever the cost. But I was terrified, and as I listened behind the curtain as the audience settled in and people laughed, coughed, and chatted, my anxiety soared even higher. I couldn't focus my concentration on Digger, couldn't crawl inside him, so I spit on the red curtain that separated the audience from me. It worked. The curtain represented the fourth wall to me—a conceptual barrier between the actors onstage and the audience—and interacting with it was a way to claim my territory. When it seemed I was in such danger of exploding that I didn't have any other choice, it helped.

By the time the curtain opened that night, my stage fright had transported me into a kind of blank space—a zone in which thinking and feeling disappeared and were replaced by the opportunity to briefly become someone else. Instead of flooring me, that blank space actually felt pretty great, and inside of it—or so I was told—I played the part of Digger as well as anyone could have imagined.

But when the curtain dropped, I had no clue about what had just transpired onstage. The troupe met for drinks after the performance, and my new cohorts replayed the evening and assured me that I had done well. Kit Carson congratulated me and wanted me to know that he had known from the moment he'd met me that I had what it took. Thanks to him, I now had a hell of a reason to get out of bed every morning, and for the next few years, Kit cast me in dozens of roles that allowed me to learn, to stretch, to grow as an actor every time the curtain went up.

He also encouraged me—no, *commanded* is a better word—to read every play by the astonishingly talented crop of American playwrights. Tennessee Williams, Arthur Miller, Eugene O'Neill, William Inge, and others opened my eyes to how powerful theatrical drama could be, and how a brilliant performance of a fine play in front of a rapt and discerning audience was perhaps the finest artistic experience a collection of people could have.

Kit taught me that acting is a precarious endeavor, one where the actor walks a razor's edge between preparation and surrender, but this never bothered me because everything in so-called real life was very precarious, too, as far as I was concerned. Something about acting made it seem precious as well—vital and worthwhile in the best sort of way—and aided me with incredible stories that I could inhabit to explore sides of myself as yet undeveloped. When Kit suggested that I needed to start working in summer stock if I was going to truly advance my talent, I immediately agreed.

Summer stock is an opportunity for actors to get their feet wet in small repertory theaters throughout the country during a summer season. With a glowing letter of recommendation from him and a phony résumé tallying *all* my acting experience, more than just the one play I had actually been in . . . I scored a position at the Little Theatre of the Rockies for the summer in Greeley, Colorado—far, far from Broadway—and I was thrilled.

The Little Theatre of the Rockies was based at the University of Northern Colorado, in a town whose nearby cattle feedlots give it the distinct aroma that is its chief source of notoriety. But the Little Theatre was renowned, too, in largest part because its director Helen Langworthy had a reputation as one of the best directors west of the Mississippi. Helen ran her program like a taskmaster, and she was a tough old broad. She was no fragile beauty, and she profoundly loved her work, frequently sitting back in the auditorium during rehearsals and barking instructions with a military bearing.

Like most newbies, my inclination was to shout my lines in hopes that they would reach the last row of the big, thousand-seat space. But yelling took me out of character, made me sound spastic, and utterly destroyed any poetry in the piece. Helen taught me the trick of simply raising my energy level and letting *it* carry my voice. She was right; it worked brilliantly, but I never became truly comfortable in a big house in the way I was in an intimate theater, and perhaps that explains why I ended up in film.

Ms. Langworthy had hired me as a lead actor who would perform in eight plays that summer, one right after the other. I was paid so little that I didn't need to bother with a bank account—fifty dollars a week and a room at a downtown Greeley flophouse—but the experience was extraordinary. I played both Biff and Willy Loman in Arthur Miller's *Death of a Salesman,* and while Biff was a natural role for me, truly becoming his defeated father was the biggest challenge I had yet faced.

But it was my role as Mio Romagna in Maxwell Anderson's *Winterset* that left a lasting impression on Helen Langworthy and the theatergoers of Greeley. Written in twentieth-century verse, the story surrounds Mio's attempt to prove his father's innocence after he is falsely convicted, then executed for robbery and murder. I dyed my hair black for the part and did my best to approximate an earnest, first-generation immigrant Italian. My own assessment was that my performance was far from stellar, but man, it was great to get so far afield from the Midwestern boy I remained off the stage, and I soared with enthusiasm for what I could accomplish onstage and how wonderful it could make me feel.

I arrived several weeks early for my second summer season in Greeley and was kicking around town when I bumped into a friend from the theater program and he approached me with what at first seemed to be a brilliant idea. It was May 1965 and the march from Selma to Montgomery had taken place just six weeks earlier. Young people across the country were on fire with newly forged commitment to the civil rights movement, and, like thousands of others from virtually every state, my buddy suggested that we travel south for a few weeks to lend a hand with the voter-registration drives that were taking place across the South. Yes, I emphatically told him, I'd join him and we'd do our small part toward setting things right in our country.

But the day before we were scheduled to drive east across Colorado's plain en route to possible danger, I backed out, tendering some excuse about needing to stay in town to ensure that all my ducks were in a row for the upcoming theater season. But the truth was that I was chickenshit. White Southerners were not taking kindly to priests and nuns and college kids coming into their cities and towns to foment trouble, as they saw it, and volunteers in many states were being harassed, beaten, even murdered in the name of keeping the South forever segregated. Dr. Martin Luther King Jr., his black constituents, and thousands of white supporters were bravely standing up against the South's— and the nation's—reprehensible racial history, but when it came time for me to rise and be counted, too, it turned out that I simply didn't have the guts to contribute.

The bright side of this episode was that it confirmed for me that I was truly an actor. What it did was finally *demand* that I question whether I could be satisfied with a life in which I was solely and completely committed to acting. Could I be happy knowing that my main contribution would be in the shared experience of theater?

The answer, I determined, was yes. I never looked back with regret at not finishing a football career, because I had found something that provided adrenaline as well as the exploration of my creative and sensitive being. I also loved the way in which once a play started, I was in total control. I understood that the stage is a world that is predetermined in many ways, one in which art shapes and gives meaning to what is otherwise terribly mundane or difficult. For me, acting had already proven to be wonderfully therapeutic. I had become an actor because real life was hard for me. Sometimes it was really rough. Acting was different from real life, yet it gave me the chance to search for complex stories that helped me understand and cope with what I encountered away from the stage lights.

Back home in Phoenix at the end of that summer, I really began to feel like I was finding my groove as an actor—and as a student, as hard as that was to believe. Kit Carson and Helen Langworthy had proven to me that teachers could rock your world, if you let them, and for the first time in my life I found myself enjoying the structure that taking classes offered. In addition to my workload at the Little Theatre, I enrolled in a few acting classes at Phoenix College, where the drama department was excellent, and where a fine director and teacher named John Paul sized me up as we rehearsed *Inherit the Wind.* The play was a tall task for college kids, but my fellow players and I relished the experience. I even found myself appreciating Mr. Paul's backhanded compliment when he suggested, "Nolte, I know you're a Method guy, but sometimes you simply must do the directed deed, interior motivation be damned." Then he added, even more to the point, "Step away from technique with this and just sing it out. Just physically do this!"

For the record, I have never considered myself a Method actor, despite borrowing liberally from Stanislavski's playbook. The Method requires you to pull out pieces of your own experience to match the emotional quality required for the work at hand. In addition to the Method, I like to think that I'm from the whatever-it-takes-to-resonate-with-a-character school. And what it took for me was a hell of a lot of hard work. My dyslexic challenges with reading turned line-learning into a hellish ordeal, for example. So, I compensated by first writing out *every* character's dialogue in longhand—not only my own. Eventually, I'd feel like *I* wrote the play, but more than that, after about a month I could begin to create my character from his words and actions on the page, my imagination, and sometimes the current experiences of my personal life. My characters would finally come into their own as we rehearsed—and this is basically how I go about my business even to this day.

I learned a ton from John Paul and his acting class and the plays we produced, but even more from Allen Dutton, a surrealistic photographer who had been a student and friend of Minor White, the hugely renowned American photographer who had recently begun to teach in the new visual arts department at the Massachusetts Institute of Technology. Both Dutton and White agreed that photography's goal was to disrupt an object's cliché in the photographer's memory bank, and instead capture a new relationship between it and how it was perceived. The effect was radically different from the pictorial style of Ansel Adams, although all three of them were enormously interested in landscapes. But Dutton and White didn't want to document beauty; what they sought was to persuade viewers to see, truly *see*, in entirely innovative ways.

Despite being way overqualified to be teaching at a community college, Allen was a terrific teacher and he had unusual patience with beginners for a man of his stature. With his help, I built a darkroom and learned open-tank film development. As obsessive as I could be back then, with my camera in hand I began to explore Phoenix like it was the most fascinating place on the planet. In the midsixties, it was still a dyed-in-the-wool frontier town, which meant from my perspective that it was full of visual delights.

Older folks around town liked to listen to country music, while the younger set loved the music of a onetime local DJ named Lee Hazlewood. He had this lonesome-drifter storytelling style that fit the desert perfectly, it seemed to me. Lee wrote songs with and produced albums for another Phoenix guy named Duane Eddy, a twangy "rebel" guitarist who was also wildly popular. Some people labeled their music "cowboy psychedelic," even though none of us had any idea what "psychedelic" meant yet. Whatever their roots, the two musicians provided me with a personal, expeditionary soundtrack on the radio while I drove.

As I explored the valley, I was drawn to barbed wire in all its myriad presentations, but foremost I liked to photograph Mexican cemeteries, where tombstones, shrines, plastic Jesuses, and fading pink plastic flowers kept me shooting images for hours on end. I was always drawn to bright colors, even though I exclusively used black and white film, maybe because I saw a powerful kind of symbolism in black and white, which could transform "reality" into something similar yet artistically very different in much the same way that a performance onstage could do.

My photographs began to make an impression on Allen, which thrilled me, and I loved the fact that in addition to being a master of his craft he was something of a skeptical jester, open to any lame-brained idea without letting the cheese slide completely off his cracker. "Life is a gag worthy of a loose solemnity," he'd say. Then another time, it was, "Nick, don't dismiss anyone or any idea. The learning curve bends in mysterious ways."

The veracity of that remark became obvious on the day he received a package from Timothy Leary and Richard Alpert, who later would become known as Ram Dass. Following their instructions and using the LSD the package supplied, we drove out into the desert; chewed little pieces of paper, then swallowed them; and crawled into our sleeping bags, from which we didn't reemerge for many hours. The drug came on in slow, rolling waves, each one unhitching superfluous gray matter as it did its magic. I noticed that I could trace the wind in my mind before I could hear or feel it. Then the earth was alive and breathing, something I thought I already knew, but I wasn't aware of the miracle's magnitude before that moment. I recognized that tumbleweeds have personalities and that flies just want to be our friends.

The LSD peaked inside me, bombarding me with images that were like splattering color on any surface I imagined. It was awe inspiring. Allen was equally moved, and soon thereafter the experience changed his entire approach to photography. He adopted a collage technique, incorporating composite imagery into his work and blending separate pictures into one layered photo before Photoshop was created.

Over that year we took five more trips together, always with wonderful results.

My takeaway was that while science represents what we know and can prove, it's up to mysticism to creatively imagine answers to the unknown. Photography and acting are both mystical endeavors in the end, aimed at helping us understand what we otherwise cannot know. I can't overstate the broadening effect Allen Dutton had on my life in those days, and how his influence has continued for decades. He taught me that creative pursuits require both space and the ability to forget what you think you know. We always need new eyes before we can rebuild anything, he was enough of a friend and mentor to help me understand.

I was cast in the role of Helen Keller's brother in the Phoenix Little Theatre's production of *The Miracle Worker* early in 1966. I was twenty-five years old. A stunning brunette named Sheila Page who was the belle of the local theater scene won the role of Annie Sullivan, the young woman responsible for Helen's breakthrough therapy. Sheila was ten years older than me, divorced with two children, and a fine actress. Following our premiere performance on a January evening, the cast joined our patrons for an opening reception. Every man who was present was shooting for Sheila.

Yet Sheila wouldn't have it. That flood of testosterone-fueled attention annoyed her enough that she took me by the arm and whispered, "You're with me now, Nick," and she kept me close by her side for the remainder of the event. I was shocked and elated but assumed she'd recruited me just to usher her through the evening.

Sheila had other intentions. Within the year, we were married by a justice of the peace. It was a perfect plan, she convinced me, and I went along without hesitation. I liked her maturity, she was sultry and mysterious and sexy as hell, and we both were actors. She didn't have to convince me much to say yes. My parents liked Sheila's sophistication and supported the marriage. Our marriage was unconventional from start to finish.

I had an easy rapport with her kids and was able to create a solid relationship with them by assuring them that I wouldn't try to replace their father in any way. I would be their older friend they could always count on and if they called, I would come. From the outset, Sheila decreed that we would have an open marriage; the free-loving sixties were in full bloom and I couldn't believe my good fortune. Our dalliances with other people seemed to suit both of us—except for the one time when we engaged in an entirely disastrous foursome. One thing I took away from that awkward night was if there isn't equal attraction among the players, the game doesn't work. In most ways our relationship was something of a dream come true for this twenty-five-year-old guy who wanted a family life but wasn't ready for one. It perfectly suited Sheila's needs as well. She had been married for ten years prior, to a strict Jewish man, and had begun to feel stifled by her life. Now she could spread her wings as an actress and build one that suited her. Soon it was time for me to return to Greeley, and Sheila and I entered a long stretch of time in which we were apart much more often than we were together.

Back in Greeley for the third summer, I was greeted with the news that our renowned director and mentor Helen Langworthy had retired. I was disappointed, but as a veteran by now, I had a say in what plays scheduled for that summer I would perform in, and John Osborne's *Luther* was irresistible. The young director was a guy named John Willcoxon; he tapped me for the challenging lead role of Martin Luther, and together we and the rest of our company pulled off something of a triumph, at least on a Colorado-sized scale.

The play is a powerful depiction of Martin Luther's life, from his spiritual crisis and anger at the Catholic Church to his instigation of the Protestant Reformation, and it's a great piece that truly tests its lead's capabilities. The British actor Albert Finney had set the bar very high with his tour-de-force 1961 performance in the play's premiere in England. Five years later in the American heartland, portraying a disaffected youth was right up my alley—I certainly understood the complexities of a nervous breakdown. But by act 3, inhabiting Luther as an old man became a monumental challenge for me. My youth and inexperience with the breadth and depths of life prevented me from really mastering that portion of Osborne's story, but I acquitted myself reasonably well.

Osborne used Luther's constipation as a metaphor for the kink in his soul. It could've been substituted for my inability to learn the lines as well. During one rehearsal, it came to a head as I flubbed another speech. Exasperated, I belly-flopped on the stage, then proceeded to pound it furiously in frustration while screaming and moaning, "I can't, I can't, I can't . . ." The young actress playing Katherine was taken aback, scolding me unsympathetically, "That's no way for an actor to behave." Willcoxon gently rose to my defense, saying, "No, Nick is right, that's exactly how Luther felt." His support led me to dust myself off and try again. I eventually was able to spit out the dialogue—not that anyone would've noticed with all the sweat gushing out of me like a fountain.

Although I didn't know until after the performance—and thank God I didn't—my dad, by himself, came to Greeley and watched a performance. *Luther* was the *only* play he ever saw me perform in. He was blown away. After the performance, with the audience cheering repeatedly at curtain call, we went out for a bite to eat at a nearby diner. "Where did that come from, Nick?" he asked, hoping to understand how I pulled the tortured complexity of Luther from inside me.

His question made clear how impressed he was—and proud—and it meant the world to me that I had done something away from the football field that affected him and made him believe his son had survived his crack-up and now was thriving. I remembered answering as if it were no big deal. "It's always been in there, Pop," I told him.

Back in Phoenix again in the fall of 1966, I was approached by a colleague, Mel Weiser, to join a new theater company called the Actors Inner Circle. I was sold on their promises of risk-taking productions and unconventional concepts. The plan was to mount twelve productions a year, like Harold Pinter's *The Caretaker* and Tennessee Williams's *Orpheus Descending,* in which I starred as Val, a young man with a guitar, a snakeskin jacket, a questionable past, and animal erotic energy. Sheila played Lady, a middle-aged woman with a dying husband who sees in Val the possibility of new life he seems to offer her, a tempting antidote to her loveless marriage and boring, small-town world. Sheila and I could be dynamic together onstage—and we often were—despite the increasing challenges that open marriage and constant separation posed. Then we were separated once more.

Mel and I received offers from Roy Disney to star in an episode of *Walt Disney's Wonderful World of Color* on television in 1968. I hadn't done any TV except for a commercial or two but I was curious, so I took the job. A production in the mountains near Flagstaff, "The Feather Farm" was an episode about a couple of ostrich ranchers and their many tribulations. It went on and on for two grueling months—largely because those funny animals refused to do as they were told. One ostrich would go left, one would go right, and the one Mel was riding would zigzag all over the place while Mel swung a little broom maniacally in an attempt to steer. Apparently, they weren't ready for prime time.

When I finally returned to Phoenix—worn out but with change in my pocket—I tried to catch up on what had been transpiring in Sheila's life, only to hear rather nonchalantly from her that she had been enjoying sex with our friend Travis.

Even though we had an agreement, I went ape-shit at the news, as things are different when close friends are involved. I think I moved in and out of our house about seven times that first week I was home. It was clear that I had a serious jealous streak inside me, no matter how open-minded I pretended to be, and my wife was not sympathetic. This was our deal, after all, she reminded me, and I finally scooped up my pride and went back to her—for a bit.

Actors Inner Circle was suddenly disbanded when Mel and Michael Byron, its codirectors, were offered Broadway jobs, dropped everything they were doing in the desert, and headed to New York City. The rest of us were left high and dry, angry as hell and uncertain about our futures. One night at a bar where several of us were trying to generate some possibilities and a good buzz, Bob Aden, a seasoned actor at the Arizona Repertory Theatre, told me that the Old Log Theatre in Excelsior, Minnesota, was looking for a lead actor. I barely knew Bob, but I guessed that he recognized a lifer when he saw one. Fate continued to shine favorably in my direction when I needed it most.

I called the Old Log's director, a guy named Don Stolz who had been running the operation since the forties. I explained my situation, asking, "What if I showed up tomorrow? Would you give me a shot?" I think he was impressed, but I was so amped up he had to interrupt, saying, "Son, what's your name?" "Oh, yeah, that's important, my name is Nick Nolte." "See you tomorrow then, Mr. Nick Nolte." I hung up, then I shared the news with Sheila that she and the kids were going to be on their own again for a while, that I needed to try it out as work had disappeared in Phoenix and this was an important opportunity. Sheila was beginning to see that our open life was expanding geographically. Her father, Lenny Page, had been the master of ceremonies at the Glen Island Casino in New Rochelle, New York, and had worked with Sinatra, Sammy Davis Jr., and the like. He had asked her early on what she was going to do when "Nick [made] it big." Apparently, he felt I had what it took and was worried about his daughter. She had shrugged and said, "We'll deal with that when it comes." It appeared the time was rapidly coming.

The Old Log Theatre, cited as one of the longest continually operating professional theaters in America, was Don Stolz's baby and had been for many years. It specialized in presenting family entertainment and light comedies and farces—precisely the sorts of productions that, at the time, I felt weren't my cup of tea. But the truth was that these plays depend on an easygoing pizzazz that just didn't come naturally to me. My stock in trade was *intensity*, but my ferocity, in fact, was a crutch, and Stolz was onto my act very early.

In one of our first rehearsals, he really gave me the business, punctuating his response to his new actor's attitude with words I'll never forget and for which I'm forever grateful. "As long as you judge these characters, Nick," he said in his plainspoken manner, "you'll never understand them." His remarks cured me of my egotism instantly, and for three excellent years in Excelsior, I learned teamwork, punctuality, and sacrifice, and I've never been tempted to try to steal the show in all the work I've done since.

The desert by now had begun to feel like home, but I remained a proud Midwesterner at heart, and because Excelsior was anchored to the shore of Lake Minnetonka, a large lake and a very fine place to fish, I thought I'd come to Mecca. The 2,500 year-round residents of Excelsior embraced me like I was a native son and I fit right in. It was wonderful.

In the middle of nowhere, but only a twenty-minute drive from the Twin Cities, the Old Log's six hundred seats were always full. I found a cool basement apartment on Main Street next door to Pete's Pizza, where I built twenty-six-inch bass-reflex stereo speakers that could make Dr. John and the Night Trippers so loud they would take your head off. I got to know lots of local kids—most of whom were a few years younger than me—and I was often found hanging in the college's commons area sewing flowers onto shirts for anyone who wanted them and getting to know the community. I met a great group of friends and together we did our best to look after boys coming home from Vietnam. After what they had been through in Southeast Asia, these soldiers' reentry into Minnesota life was never easy, and we would do what we could to help by hijacking them at the airport before their families knew they were back, then keeping them safe, surrounded by the buddies they had known all their life and full of booze, until they settled in and were ready to try home life once more.

Sheila made a few visits here and there that year—but only briefly on breaks from my responsibilities at the Old Log, as I was ultimately a member of the company in Excelsior for three full seasons. Although we missed each other, our relationship had always had a fated feeling to it, as if we both knew it served us deeply yet was for a limited time. When I was offered a Prestone antifreeze commercial that was scheduled to shoot in New York, I phoned Sheila, and she wanted me to come home to Phoenix, but I flew east instead. On my arrival, however, I learned that filming the ad had been postponed for six weeks. I knew I should return home and face her, let us go our inevitable separate ways, but I chickened out and focused on my next job. I did some modeling and audited the acting classes of Sandy Meisner and Stella Adler, both of whom deserved their reputations as extraordinary teachers. I remember Stella explaining to a young actress who was struggling with a Tennessee Williams role. "No, no, no, dear," she told her, "with Tennessee, we've got to *wear* the poetry." That seemed to me excellent advice no matter who the playwright. To be a good actor, you must wear the poetry, the rhythm, as if they are your clothes.

Before I left New York, as a way to help keep my head above water, I did a Clairol print commercial with a young blond model. The ad for Clairol's "Summer Blonde" was such a hit that the company later used the photograph—the two of us mugging on a piece of driftwood—on the box of dye itself, the only time a guy's ever appeared on a woman's hair-color package, as far as I know.

At last, however, it was time to return to Arizona, as Sheila had sent me divorce papers. She had the divorce all figured out, just like the marriage. Sheila came over to the ramshackle desert rat's spread I had rented on several desolate acres and said, "I have thought this all out. You don't have anything and I don't have much—but it will be all clear, all you have to do is sign." Then, as things happen, we ended up falling into bed one last time. Instead of a nostalgic romp, however, it turned madcap as a large wooden sculpture above the bed fell down and hit her on the head. It was just one of those embarrassing, crazy moments. The last go, and boom! We had had a great ten years; I learned a lot from her and we played many roles across from each other. I brought her ice and we both shared a bittersweet laugh.

I moved out the remaining items I had in her house and I continued to see Sheila's son, and because my parents were living in Phoenix by the early seventies, Sheila and my mother remained close for many years. But the two of us were done; we both knew it, accepted it, and moved on.

———

It was early in 1972 when destiny stepped into my life again. Keith Anderson, a Phoenix-based director I knew, got in touch to say that he and Bob Johnson, producer of the city's new Southwest Ensemble Theatre, were planning the world premiere of renowned playwright William Inge's *The Last Pad*. It's set in a prison's death row on a night when a young man is scheduled to be electrocuted. Keith had me in mind for Jess, the lead, a wife-killer who is living his last hours. I desperately wanted the role before I'd even read the play. Inge was a master, one of contemporary America's great playwrights, and I hadn't had a role this meaty, this challenging, this consequential in a very long time. And a world premiere! My God, this was why—already into my thirties—I continued to be committed to this craft that had rather literally saved my life more than a decade before.

A Kansan by birth and the recipient of the 1953 Pulitzer Prize for his play *Picnic*, Inge examined the human condition with subtle penetration. Yet Inge never achieved the fame he sought, and he always struggled personally with his closeted homosexuality.

Early in the 1970s, Inge was teaching playwriting at the University of California at Irvine and sinking ever deeper into depression. With *The Last Pad*, he appeared to be making a conscious decision to kill off his archetypal characters, each of whom was also a side of himself. Jess, the role I would play, is very reminiscent of Inge's character Hal in *Picnic*, a young man who pretends boldness and confidence yet is ready to collapse in defeat and self-doubt. The two other inmates scheduled to die are a cynical gay inmate and an old philosopher who is the only member of the trio who can simply accept his fate.

Two fine fellow actors, Jim Matz and Richard Elmore, joined me onstage when we opened very inauspiciously at the Kerr Cultural Center in Scottsdale before moving to the Unitarian Church in Phoenix when the play proved to be a big hit and our run was extended. Inge himself drove over to see us perform when word reached him that we were doing a hell of a job, and he was hugely enthusiastic about what he saw. "You guys have just nailed this," he gushed, and soon he insisted that we find a way to bring the play to Los Angeles.

I was still in the shacklike house in the desert on two and a half acres, hanging out with local Indians and wandering with my dogs alone. I had developed a relationship with castor beans. Castor beans could grow anywhere and if you have ten feet of them, you have a canopy that is dark and twenty degrees cooler than the Arizona heat. Mom came to visit after the initial Phoenix success of *The Last Pad* and we sat out on beat-up old chairs in our own private jungle. No one could hear us and there was blood dripping off every other tree from blood bags that a couple of local nurses would give me, as blood meal is great nutrition for the plant.

She said, "So this is the way you are going to go. To L.A.?"

I was likely going to go; I knew having an invitation would change everything. I knew it for sure. And just to play around with her, I said, "Well, I don't know. I might stay with these castor beans, it sure is peaceful." She smiled, not letting me get her goat at all. If anybody knew about tempo and rhythm, the time when you should do things and the time when you are out of sync, it was her. My mother believed in destiny. We both knew I was going.

Our production moved to Los Angeles in the early summer of 1973 and opened at the prestigious Contempo Theatre, now the Geffen, in Westwood, on June 15. Little did we know that tragedy would hit just four days before we opened, as Inge killed himself by carbon monoxide poisoning. Some say he orchestrated his departure to help give his beloved final creation a bit more attention. *The Last Pad* is a very fine play in its own right, but the world lost a brilliant voice the day Inge took his life. We were deeply shaken, and I'm sure that added a level of intensity to our performances of his last work.

By the second week of our run, the good buzz made sure we were sold out for dozens of weeks to come, *Time* magazine was doing a story, and agents were swarming around. Actors like Elizabeth Taylor and Sidney Poitier were attending, then coming backstage to say hello. But I wanted no part of that—I simply would not open my dressing-room door, no matter *who* wanted to see me.

Finally, my old friend and acting coach Bryan O'Byrne, who had lit the first spark of interest in acting in me long ago in Laurel Canyon, came to the playhouse and tried to talk some sense into me. I explained to Bryan that I was shy, and what in the hell did I have to say to Elizabeth Taylor anyway?

"That's ridiculous!" Bryan laughed. "Everybody is *shy*, for Christ's sake. You can't do this anymore, Nick. All they want to do is congratulate you. Of course you don't know Elizabeth Taylor, goddamn it. Just be gracious to her."

That posthumous production of Inge's *The Last Pad* was about to change everything for me professionally, and like I'd done with Kit Carson and Helen Langworthy and John Willcoxon and Don Stolz and many other mentors in regional theaters around the country over the previous decade, I did my best to truly take Bryan's wise words to heart. At the Contempo Playhouse, I continued to act my ass off as Jess, the convict condemned to die, and I didn't move away from Southern California ever again.

Chapter 7
Rich Man

ABC struggled mightily in its ratings war against its competing networks in the mid-1970s—and it regularly lost. But its position as the nation's underdog network led legendary television producer Fred Silverman, who joined the network as head of ABC Entertainment in 1975, to take some big risks in hopes that things might turn around. He approved a project planned as a brand-new concept for television. It was going to be called "movies for television," a multiple-hour television drama whose entire run would last just a few weeks. The first series Silverman wanted to create was based on a very popular novel by Irwin Shaw titled *Rich Man, Poor Man,* a story that followed the divergent lives of two brothers whose parents were impoverished German immigrants to the U.S.

Early on, the producers thought that Peter Strauss, a successful young actor who had appeared in several recent series, would be ideal as Rudy Jordache, the ambitious brother. And although I was much less well-known, director Hank Schloss, whom I had worked with on a number of small film projects, fought hard on my behalf to convince the producers of the series that I would be the perfect choice to play Tom, the rebellious brother who fails at most everything.

In the two years since *The Last Pad* had made such a mark on the Los Angeles theater scene, Bryan O'Byrne had been pumping *The Last Pad* reviews onto casting directors' desks left and right and people wanted to see what I looked like on film. As a result, I'd gotten cast in some fun little television and film roles, including episodes of *Barnaby Jones, Cannon, Gunsmoke,* and *Electra Glide in Blue,* in which I played the part of a hippie—without any credit.

By the time *Rich Man, Poor Man* was announced, I had gotten a little repute; the William Morris Agency was hot on me. But they held off on signing me so I went with another agency. I had an agent, Lou Pitt—whose clients included Arnold Schwarzenegger, Bruce Lee, Dudley Moore, and Jessica Lange—and a manager, Mimi Weber, who once had represented Laurence Olivier and Cary Grant and now was managing newcomers like me who were trying their luck at the business. I had worked with a director at Universal who brought me in without an interview for the role of Tom—and I *wanted* it. The buzz about the ABC project was *big,* and I had set my eye on it.

On the day they screen-tested me, I was matched with Strauss, whom I hadn't met before. We went over our lines for a while, then gave it our best shot in front of the studio guys, and I was already so far into the role that I knew we had just nailed it. As we walked to our cars I told him I looked forward to seeing him when we started shooting. He reminded me that we hadn't been given the parts yet, but I knew better. "Hey, it's going to happen," I told him. "We're doing this thing." And so we did.

Rich Man is a rangy piece, and the true challenge for both of us was that we had to portray our characters from teens to middle age. Tom, my character, goes from sixteen to forty-five, and it was playing a rank teenager that gave me some pause. During rehearsals, I paid attention to the ways in which Peter lightened his voice and shifted some of his mannerisms as a way to become younger, but I was sure that approach wouldn't work for me. I was thirty-five! I looked young but not *that* young, so I spent a lot of time trying to access the true qualities of youth before it came to me that—in addition to dropping my weight down to the 150 pounds I carried when I played high school ball—I simply had to react to the world I encountered. Kids don't think; they just react. Tom is a reactionary, and he's troubled, and I began to understand him very well.

Man, I must have run around the Hollywood Reservoir a thousand times to get my weight down—even in the middle of the night. And to help me express Tom's teenage malaise, I put cotton in my ears so it seemed I was deep in my adolescent fog. At least that's what I did until Dorothy McGuire, who played Tom's mother, found me out and threw a fit, telling me in no uncertain terms that the cotton was a trick, and that actors—*good* actors—didn't use tricks. I rolled my eyes like a teenager and continued on in my fog.

The early buzz was astounding—so much so that ABC decided to reshape the production just as we began shooting. A huge audience by today's standards was expected; this was still an era of rabbit-ears antennae and only a handful of channels. The suits believed it was a critical point in television, and they could reposition themselves among the competition while making bundles of money from advertisers. When I was hired, my contract had stipulated my performance in three two-hour movies that would air on three separate nights.

But soon after we began shooting, producer Jon Epstein called me in to say, "Look, Nick, this stuff is so good we want to stretch it out. We think it's so captivating that we can stretch it to twelve one-hour shows."

I told Jon I wasn't a fan of that idea. I thought making the change would diminish it terribly—the show would seem just like any other TV show if it ran for only an hour each week. But he worked hard to convince me, assuring me that the production was going to be something special, the kind of thing that never had been done before. No single episode would stand alone; all of them would be part of a cohesive narrative arc. It was the first time I remember hearing the term "miniseries."

Irwin Shaw, author of the novel, disliked the plan, too. He was upset enough that the tension between him and the studio was palpable, yet he didn't bolt and he continued to oversee the scripting of each hour—and the writing remained excellent. For my part, I decided just to go back to work and try to make the role of Tom Jordache my best performance yet, and the hard work that all of us put into the show really paid off. *Rich Man, Poor Man* was spectacularly successful; ABC's stature as a network was transformed forever, and Fred Silverman was made out to be something of a genius.

I always used to drink beer. And that was against the rules at work. But I'd drink beer. When it was time to shoot the final episode, I decided to prepare by drinking a ton. My final scene called for me to be drunk, and I had decided to play it while I was shit-faced. It was a great scene, and I didn't miss a beat, but evidently some of the studio executives had come down to watch the final shoot and they were not happy to find me inebriated.

Once we wrapped, director David Greene and I were sitting on our butts in a studio alley drinking a celebratory beer, and David told me that the producers weren't happy with me, adding that I was good enough that I hadn't needed to get drunk to play Tom as a convincing drunk. I told David I knew that, but I added that I wanted my last work on the show to be special, and so I'd simply decided to turn to the beer.

Not long after, the suits at Universal announced that henceforth no actor in a drinking scene would be allowed to consume alcohol. It seemed silly to me, but that's what they decreed—likely because of me. By the time the final episode aired—on an evening when the United States Congress was meeting in closed session—interest in the miniseries was so huge that the legislators were interrupted by the announcement, "Tom Jordache was killed by Falconetti on ABC tonight."

Evidently, no one informed the elected officials that both Tom Jordache and Nick Nolte had been drunk when the crime was committed.

If my performance in William Inge's *The Last Pad* had gotten me back to Hollywood, it was my role as Tom in *Rich Man, Poor Man* that fundamentally changed my life as an actor. I'd been offered a very fine part and I'd created a character who was rebellious, hyperactive, irresponsible, yet filled with overpowering emotion. After thirteen years as a professional actor, I was pronounced an "overnight sensation"; my stock rose sky-high, and I was in immediate demand for an array of intriguing new roles. But I was wary of Hollywood and losing myself in the falsehood of fame, so I retreated to my childhood sanctuary of nature and got the hell outta Dodge.

I'd found a fantastic old house about twenty miles west of Los Angeles in an empty expanse of grassy brown hills and scattered California oaks near the spot where Triunfo Canyon Road met Kanan Road in what is now called Agoura Hills. Almost as soon as I saw the place—a big Normandy-style house with gun sights built into the basement by an eccentric German who'd been convinced that the Nazis would win World War II—I knew I wanted to live there, and that it would ground me. I quickly purchased it with money I'd earned from *Rich Man, Poor Man.*

My manager, Mimi Weber, was not pleased. She was certain that because of my television star turn she now had quite a hot property on her hands, and she informed me that I could *not* move away from L.A. I explained that twenty miles west was hardly "away," and that it was a straight shot east on the 101 freeway to the Burbank studios. I could get to work in thirty minutes—back in an era before the 101 became a virtual parking lot a couple of times each day—and that was less time than it often took to drive to the studios from Laurel Canyon or many other in-town locations.

In the end, there wasn't a damn thing Mimi could do about where I chose to call home, and it *was* as easy for me to get to the studios—especially when I raced to town on my motorcycle via the Mulholland Highway, a killer stretch of dirt road in those days that I would ride as fast as I could. One night I did flip my 500 cc Triumph and ended up in some guy's yard, the bike still running and in gear and grinding up his grass. I popped both heels off the cowboy boots I was wearing, but otherwise I was fine. I got the bike up and mounted it again and made it back to the ranch hardly the worse for wear.

Steve McQueen, a far better motorcyclist than me,

was part owner of a place nearby, one he used primarily as a destination—just to see how quickly he could reach it via Decker Canyon Road, up and over the mountains on his bike from his main house on Broad Beach in Malibu. He could make the trip in something like eight minutes, he said, which meant he was taking hairpin turns at an ungodly crazy speed, and it was Steve and his biker mystique that ultimately turned those canyon roads into the motorcycle mecca they remain.

There was something special about living in the country in those days and I loved its back-of-beyond feel. I shared the big house with a regular gaggle of hippie friends who followed me out from Excelsior and would crash for a few nights or a few weeks. This little commune included a gal named Karen Eklund, who became an on-again-off-again girlfriend for several years, as well as my longtime pal Rocky. Throughout my life, I have always thrived in an open home where friends could come and go. A little chaos around keeps me sane.

Friends ground me, too, and Rocky was one such special soul, an innocent who wrote in hieroglyphics and wandered the hills with my dogs. He wasn't allowed to have a driver's license, but he could legally drive on my property, of course, and we had lots of fun on the off-road motorbikes I bought for everyone to play with. We also enjoyed sneaking out under the cover of darkness to shoot out the lights that the road department was installing alongside Kanan Road as it was widened into four lanes. The development of the road and those goddamn bright lights meant we were losing our little Eden, and it was wicked fun to destroy them as soon as they went up, at least until the day when a SWAT team appeared in the area, determined to find out which vengeful mountain folk were destroying the state of California's property. A few years later, I found out that Rocky had died in a fire in a little squatter's cabin he had built down the road. It breaks my heart to this day. I still feel the sting of responsibility for being the pied piper who drew those kids out from Excelsior to L.A. I know we each choose our own path, but Rocky and I had shared one and I wish I could have protected him.

It wasn't unusual to have friends and colleagues from the film industry drive out to visit. I'm sure many of them thought I was a bit deranged to want to live so far from the action—yet others were quite impressed by the Agoura countryside and its lack of any pretense. Peter Strauss, my *Rich Man, Poor Man* costar, was so taken by the area, in fact, that he asked me to help him find a place of his own.

I knew of a twenty-acre ranch for sale, a place

where a bunch of hippies were crashing, just across the road from the store and tavern McQueen had helped Tom Runyon open in 1970 out of the ruins of Hank's Country Store and the old Cornell post office building. Runyon called his new place the Old Place, and it was special. Peter settled in nearby, and I was just up the road, and we all used to gather at the Old Place to play horseshoes and eat steaks and drink late into the night.

The success of *Rich Man* opened many a door. Offers poured in. Unfortunately, they generally were crap. Studios attempted to lure me with a succession of three-picture deals, but when I would ask about the scripts on which those movies would be created, the studio suits would say, "Don't worry about it, Nick."

I was smart enough to know that multipicture contracts were career killers, so I just bided my time at the ranch, despite the fact that I was developing the kind of reputation you don't really want to have. When producer David Susskind asked me to star in *Fort Apache*, I read the 340-page script in which nothing really happened, and then I told him no. Susskind wasn't accustomed to being turned down, and he had offered me a million dollars—real money in those days—a rejection that led him to publicly muse, "Who does this Nick Nolte think he is, turning down a million dollars?"

There was an offer on the film *Superman,* but I shut it down quickly. I said, "If I can play him as he truly is, a schizophrenic, I will do it." They were floored. I said his change of personalities makes him a schizophrenic hero. Luckily, that scared them off, as I didn't want to walk around in a muscle suit anyway.

The producers of a film called *The Deep* pitched me with a handsome offer. But my answer was again no, something that drove my manager, Mimi Weber, wild with frustration. I'd already made her crazy by turning down an opportunity to star in the sequel to *Rich Man, Poor Man,* but for God's sake, who was I going to play? They had killed off my character Tom Jordache, and no, thank you, I was not going to come back from the fucking dead!

What I wanted was to find a piece with real artistic merit, and there were three upcoming films I had my eye on. The first was *Slap Shot,* and I was a Paul Newman fan, but I couldn't manage to go from recreational ice skater to professional hockey player. Director George Roy Hill was kind enough to give me a couple months to learn, but I just couldn't get the hang of it and I lost the part. William Friedkin was set to direct *Sorcerer,* and he took the time to meet me. But as soon as I sat down, he told me he'd already cast Roy Scheider in the role that would have been mine. Strike two.

Francis Ford Coppola's talent and track record attracted every up-and-coming actor in Hollywood when his film *Apocalypse Now* was announced. I felt I was a perfect fit, but the audition was a damn doozy. It was held in a warehouse and the massive group of incredible talent was required to improvise in front of our competition. I watched Sam Elliott, Tommy Lee Jones, Martin Sheen, and many others, and as I sat the pressure grew overwhelming. At a certain point, I approached Francis and requested some beer to cut the tension.

Sure enough, trash barrels full of ice and cold cans of beer appeared in no time. It helped all of us loosen up and begin to free ourselves. Hours later and quite loose, I drove home without a clue as to how I'd done. Coppola's sister, Talia Shire, with whom I'd acted in *Rich Man, Poor Man,* telephoned the night before it was announced to tell me it looked like I'd gotten the part, but she turned out to be very wrong. I must admit I was disappointed when Harvey Keitel (later replaced by Martin Sheen) got the role instead of me. Decades later, Francis sent me a video recording of my audition, and it was still a strong audition.

The sequel to *Rich Man, Poor Man* was about to be broadcast—without *me*—and I was beginning to feel the pressure to find a new film when I decided to have my agent circle back to *The Deep,* which was based on a popular Peter Benchley novel. I was concerned the story was beyond redemption, and I felt a bit of a sell-out, but Peter Island in the British Virgin Islands was paradise, the surrounding sea was some of the clearest and most exquisite water in the world, and my scuba instructor was an expat from Texas who had me diving confidently in no time.

By the time the full cast and crew arrived, the script was getting an on-set rewrite, and although I was hopeful, my attitude continued to stink on the afternoon when we did a full read-through. I was sitting at the bar when in walked Tom Mankiewicz, the screenwriter who'd been hired to salvage the thing, and I threw my copy of the script, yelling, "There isn't a character in this whole goddamned thing!" There was an awkward silence.

Robert Shaw, the British character actor whom American audiences had recently gotten to know in *Jaws*, came over and put his arm around me, saying, "It's a *treasure* picture, Nick," then he added, "Come on back to my place. We'll have a jar and read my novels and it'll be fine."

I didn't know at the time that, in addition to his success as an actor, Shaw was an award-winning novelist and playwright, nor did I understand that a "jar" was a full pint of straight vodka poured into a glass tumbler.

He was an epic drinker—who would be dead in a couple of years—and after he had shared a page or two from one of his novels, we simply sat and talked and drank several jars. Like me, Shaw had been older when he had finally broken through in the business, and he had watched his contemporaries, like Peter O'Toole, Albert Finney, and Richard Harris, become international stars while he languished for thirty-nine episodes in a forgettable British TV series called *The Buccaneers*.

Yet Shaw had learned how to enjoy himself; he was determined to have a hell of a good time in the islands, and he suggested that I simply relax and join him. I was wise enough to take his advice, and in celebration of my change of attitude, the next day I mooned Peter Benchley, who was the credited screenwriter despite Tom Mankiewicz's recent work. On my left butt cheek, I'd had my makeup man write "The" in big, grease-penciled letters, and on the right, he'd written "Deep." Benchley seemed to think it was very funny, and I was determined to fully enjoy the rest of the shoot.

Although I now had the film in the right perspective, which made the shoot easier for everybody, we had other serious problems. The water was the clearest seawater in all the world, but film technology wasn't up to par yet. Because of the depth, the scenes looked dark and opaque once on film. This was very much a treasure picture, as Shaw said, a *diving* picture, and if it was going to be successful, our underwater scenes had to be exquisite and groundbreaking. Our British cinematographer, Chris Challis, had an idea. He flew to London to pursue the fix he had in mind, then was back on Peter Island in about a week with a bank of waterproofed ten-thousand-watt lights.

Chris's plan was simply to light up the whole fucking ocean, plain and simple. On the first day that underwater filming resumed, he tossed a couple of lights into the water and flipped a switch. They worked! It was time for us to start shooting, but not *one* of us was willing to get into the water. Our chances of getting electrocuted appeared awfully high. Exasperated with our gutlessness, Chris himself finally dove in. He swam over to the lights, adjusted them, dragged them with him as he moved about, and fully convinced us it was safe to return to the water. We went back to work and the test shots looked incredible the following day—no one had ever shot underwater footage as beautifully before.

But if Chris saved *The Deep*, Jacqueline Bisset made it a success. Her see-through white T-shirt transformed derivative schlock into a blockbuster. If people remember the movie at all, we can thank Jackie. Her T-shirt clings to her like a second skin as she climbs out of the water. It was the talk of the movie trade for a long while, and Peter Guber commented for years afterward that that T-shirt had made him a rich man.

Moviemaking is a bonding experience. People from the most disparate backgrounds imaginable come together, build an alternate universe, and inhabit it until the shoot is complete—after a month, often after six months or even more. You end up getting close to people you otherwise wouldn't meet in a million years. Throw in an exotic, faraway location and the real world feels like a past life. Working on *The Deep,* we spent six months in a virtual paradise; we were practically naked every day, we had tons of downtime, we were unsupervised adults—and people were bound to mingle.

Sparks began to fly between Jackie and me early on, and then a very groovy romance bloomed. She was more than just gorgeous and classy—she was a great sport. But Jackie called things off before we finished shooting, saying I slept with every girl on the island. It was an accusation that didn't seem fair, particularly because she flew off as often as she could manage to spend time with her French boyfriend. But we ended our tryst amicably and remained friends despite the many challenges of the remote location, the underwater work, our skin being burned and coarsened by overexposure to the sun, fire-coral rash, and our GI tracts being bombarded by parasites.

Peter Yates was an English gentleman, someone who never appeared bothered by my pranks. He supported me patiently throughout the shoot, and I appreciated it. Renowned for his direction of the series *The Saint* on British TV, he went on to direct many films and he was also the catalyst for a satisfying turn in my career when he invited his friend Karel Reisz to visit the set while we were shooting *The Deep.*

Karel was with us on a day when something went wrong and we had to endure one of our seemingly constant technical delays. I got into a foam-gun war with some guys in the prop department. The guns were designed to simulate the foam of an agitated ocean, and we turned them on each other, creating a crazy mess. As I finally walked away from the monkey business, Karel approached me, introduced himself, then asked if I'd read *Dog Soldiers.* I said yes, adding that Robert Stone was an author I very much admired. Hearing that, Karel explained that he was going to direct the film based on the Vietnam novel, then added, "I'd like you to play Ray Hicks for me."

I couldn't believe what I was hearing, and I wanted to seal the deal before he thought better of the idea. I put out my hand as I said, "Well, I tell you, Karel, I would really like to do it. I don't want to continue to do these big, gigantic films like this. I want to do meatier work."

We agreed to meet in Los Angeles after *The Deep* wrapped, and I was so filled with adrenaline that I could have sprinted a lap around the entire island. But Karel wanted to say something else before we parted. "You know, Nick, I'm going to ask you to find a real quiet place in yourself when we work together," he said calmly and very directly, "because you're wasting energy, and we're going to need to put that on-screen. If you engage with the crew too much, you give your energy to them and it doesn't get on the screen. That's just something to think about."

I understood, and we said goodbye. Our final weeks in the Caribbean were uneventful. I did my job and I couldn't wait to go home, because the role of a lifetime awaited.

Following its release, *The Deep* became a smash hit despite being panned by the critics. As I had feared, the critics clobbered me, saying I was just a "blonde cutout," "another pretty boy," and an actor with "no depth"—pun intended. Sometimes life makes choices for you that turn out better than you'd make for yourself. *The Deep* was one of those times for me.

I'd had an amazing experience in the Caribbean, and I'd successfully made the leap from television to film despite the shitty reviews—and my next film was going to be one of which I was very proud. Not bad for six months' work. Providence had smiled on me again.

Chapter 8
A Quiet Place

Karel Reisz stayed at the Chateau Marmont in Hollywood when he flew in from London to meet with the producers of *Dog Soldiers*. He telephoned me, wanting to get together to talk at length about Ray Hicks, the character I was going to play, so I cruised into town on one of my big bikes. Mulholland Highway was still a dusty road, and helmet laws were still a ways off. When I reached the hotel, the wind and dirt had turned my hair into a madman's, and Karel said he loved the look. I would still have to search for both the physical and interior essences of Ray Hicks, and right from that moment I knew he could help me find them.

Karel was a Czech who had narrowly escaped the Nazis before his parents perished in Auschwitz. Although he studied natural sciences at Cambridge, Karel became fascinated by film, making his first documentaries in the late 1950s, then moving to feature films when he produced *This Sporting Life*, starring Richard Harris. Harris was electric in it, and the movie knocked my socks off. I was thrilled that Karel wanted me to star in his new picture.

When I'd met him in the islands, I'd liked him right from the start and somehow knew I could trust him implicitly. As we talked at the hotel in the Hollywood Hills, he pinpointed the challenges that playing Ray—a merchant marine who agrees to help a disillusioned war correspondent smuggle heroin from Saigon to San Francisco during the Vietnam War—would present to me, then suggested techniques that would help me immensely in the end. "Hicks will require stillness," he calmly stressed that day. He was very aware of my tendency to make twitchy gesticulations, and he coached me on how to corral it. "Just sit there and talk. Don't use your hands," he insisted—and he was right.

He was relentless, but I was uncharacteristically receptive to the drilling because it came from the right place. This was no power trip. He taught me to focus my attention on a visual spot, then transfer it to a single thought. It sounds simple, and it might be for some, but it wasn't for me. I worked at it, and eventually I could pull it off as the cameras rolled.

In turn, I introduced Karel to Topanga Canyon, a real *Dog Soldiers* kind of locale. Mountains separate the San Fernando Valley from Los Angeles County's beach communities. Tucked into the middle, Topanga Canyon and its residents were considered the mountains' soulful epicenter by many people who knew and loved the place. Others referred to it as a hippie haven or called it the "commune corridor." Personally, I've always been attracted to the ramshackle ingenuity of these "mountain people."

In the novel, Robert Stone describes "canyon consciousness" that includes some pretty shaky morality, and he wasn't wrong. Stone's character Ray Hicks is neither a druggie nor a believer in the counterculture. His rebellion comes from a simple fear of being forced into a box that doesn't fit him—more than a bit like me, I'd wager, and I told Karel so as I drove him around in my 1948 International Harvester truck.

That wonderful old rig's gearbox wasn't synchromeshed, so we settled into a jolty and jostling ride. We navigated dozens of roads and trails that wound into and around Topanga. Karel was carsick much of the time, but that didn't stop him from declaring that Hicks would have to drive a similar truck in the movie. We ended up using a beat-up old Land Rover, which suited me fine, and the whole experience with

Karel and the film filled me with a sense of purpose and direction.

None of us liked it much that the film was ultimately titled *Who'll Stop the Rain*—a reference to the Creedence Clearwater Revival song that was one of many Creedence hits that filled the soundtrack. When the movie premiered in 1978 I got the first good film review of my career. "An actor I never expected to praise gives a smashing performance," David Denby wrote in the *New York Times*.

Who'll Stop the Rain was only a modest success at the box office, but it was an important film for me because I was able to display some depth as an actor and a complexity far beyond what *The Deep* had revealed. They didn't sell the picture well—it should have been a real hit given how the war continued to eat at our collective consciousness, the excellence of Stone's story, and the splendid work that Karel and actors Michael Moriarty and Tuesday Weld brought to the film. I wasn't morose about how the film fared, however, because I was proud of how I had inhabited Ray Hicks. And for that, I thank Karel Reisz.

Chapter 9
Something to See

Even more than football or acting, women have been the major passion of my life. I'm fascinated by them. Totally fascinated. And fascinated by myself in relation to them. Of course, men and women play a lot of games—fighting, testing. Some is for the sake of *aliveness,* but sometimes it heads toward *destruction.* But I love the fascination, love that relationship psyche. Beginning with the time when Kathy Carney captured my heart, then broke it in high school, I've been fascinated, too, by the sometimes strange and curious ways in which I relate to the women I love. I've often shown my women parts of me I'm not proud of. Yet I've felt wonderfully alive when I've been in love, even when that aliveness has taken a turn toward something destructive.

My sporadic girlfriend of several years Karen Eklund and I began to encounter real trouble during the time we lived at the ranch and my career as a film actor was taking off. I had met Karen in Minnesota when I was mesmerized by her walking across the commons in a flowing white dress. She was part of the Excelsior group of friends who had followed me and occasionally lived out at the ranch. She had a history of being sort of a grifter and possessed a kind of wildness that could sometimes make me look like a choirboy.

Though I was initially intrigued by her wildness, we weren't really a couple and I finally told Karen to move out. I wanted her to leave—end of story. She wasn't at all happy but later decided that $4.5 million in palimony would make her feel a lot better. She claimed she had been instrumental in my success and hired lawyers to file suit on her behalf. I believe it may have been only the second or third palimony suit in California, after Lee Marvin's.

It would be several years before the suit would finally be settled, but I soon became intrigued by a woman again. One evening I was in town with my friend Dino Conti at Carlos'n Charlie's, a restaurant and discotheque on Sunset Boulevard. As we surveyed the action, Dino asked if any of the women we were observing interested me. I pointed to a young blonde who was bouncing all over the place and he nodded, then went over to her and whispered something in her ear. I never heard precisely what he said, but the young woman soon walked over to me and introduced herself. "Hi, I'm Sharyn," she said.

"You have nice, sleek legs," I told her.

"Thanks. Now give me a smile, sucker," she responded, and before long the woman whom I soon began to call Legs and I decided to drive to the ranch in her car. She had some coke with her, which certainly kept the night rolling, and from that evening on we were inseparable.

Legs was a city girl, however, and life out in the country cramped her style. I had to admit that she just didn't look right standing in her little short-shorts and platform heels in a circle of the long-haired hippies who commonly hung out at the ranch smoking joints. So we moved to town, and nine months later, I called her from Phoenix, where I had been scouting movie locations, and proposed to her over the phone.

"Let's go for it," I said encouragingly, and although Legs thought I was kidding, she flew over to join me. To convince her that I was serious, I chartered a plane to Las Vegas, where the pilot and his girlfriend were our witnesses at our $70 wedding at the Chapel of the Bells. I loved Legs and wanted to be married to her; I had the old-fashioned notion that the relationship couldn't take either of us any further unless we were husband and wife. We struggled sometimes—she was fourteen years younger and very independent—but I found a kindred spirit in Legs. She was just as rowdy as I was.

One day I was talking to Barbara Hand, my assistant at the time, in her office, and on the desk there was a picture lying upside down. I flipped the picture over and there was Legs at one of my movie premieres, twirling in a skirt with no underwear on. "Oh my God. How many of these did we have to bury?"

She said, "A lot, otherwise the *Enquirer* would have published them."

I don't know how much we had to pay during those years, but Legs would not wear underwear. I guess it was erotic in the cocaine days, but Jesus Christ. You don't need to show it to the whole goddamn United States.

It was a wild era, and for a couple of years coke ensured that everything was fast, furious, and crazy—I partook in the fun, too, don't get me wrong. Like the time we left a party late one night and randomly decided it was the perfect moment to drive up to the hills to visit Jack Nicholson. We had no idea it was four in the morning, but the guard at his gate told us it was too damn early for a visit and turned the sprinklers on us.

Deciding to let Jack sleep, we drove away, soaked to the skin and laughing like hyenas.

Producer Arthur Krim had recently formed Orion Pictures with Eric Pleskow and Mike Medavoy, with whom he had worked at United Artists. The three men had guided that studio to three consecutive Oscars for best picture of the year—*One Flew over the Cuckoo's Nest* in 1975, *Rocky* in 1976, and *Annie Hall* in 1977. Krim possessed a very sharp-eyed understanding of the cultural importance of storytelling. The goal was to tap into an archetypal myth to get audiences to flock to see a story on a screen.

On the telephone one day, Arthur asked, "Nick, what do you think about the Beats?" I'm not sure how the words jumped out of me in answer to him, but I said something like, "Well, sometimes cultures exist within a larger culture that beat with a truer vibration."

He must have liked how that sounded, because he followed it with a brief pitch. "I have a wonderful piece called *Heart Beat*, Nick. It's written by Carolyn Cassady, Neal Cassady's wife. I want you to play Neal, but the director just thinks you're that hunk from *The Deep*. His name is John Byrum. Go to his house. Convince him you're Cassady."

Byrum lived on Franklin Avenue in Los Angeles at

the foot of the Hollywood Hills, and he wasn't exactly elated to see me when I knocked on his door, as Krim had instructed. "John, Arthur suggested we have a chat," I offered.

He warily let me in; we sat down and we shared some coke I'd brought along, then I did my thing. John was familiar with *Who'll Stop the Rain* but unaware that I'd played Ray Hicks, and that single detail seemed to change the tone of our meeting pretty quickly. We ended up on his roof, where I embellished my many exploits over the years in places like Omaha, Arizona, Mexico, and Southern California. I wove impressive yarns only partially fabricated as the hours passed; a whole night passed, in fact, and at some point, John finally announced, "Jesus, all right, all right! You really *are* Neal Cassady." As pleased as I was, I had to tell Byrum as I was leaving, "You know, John, you're gonna take a lot of flak for this film."

Sure enough, when word spread that we were bringing Carolyn's memoir of her life with her husband and Jack Kerouac to the screen, the surviving Beats began to carp. Allen Ginsberg made it known that he'd shut us down if we used his poetry. Ken Kesey was traveling with the Grateful Dead in Egypt, from which location he labeled us "Hollywood necrophiliacs," which seemed to me like a ridiculous thing to say except that

I very much admired Kesey's extraordinary novels and thought he was one guy who could get away with saying whatever he damn well wanted.

Neal was precious to the Beats. They'd been wowed by him, fallen in love with him, and mythologized him after his death. In some ways, Carolyn was a Yoko Ono–like figure, not so much because she stole Neal from his friends, but because instead she forced them to reckon with his humanity. Yes, he was a free-spirited, sexually liberated nonconformist. He also battled serious addiction issues and harbored a deep, secret yearning for the home he never knew. These less glamorous traits didn't support the myth, one that turned him into a caricature of himself. Carolyn loved Neal in his entirety, and I deeply respected that, hoping that we could explore not only the mythological side of Neal but also the personal side that Carolyn knew like no one else.

I personally identified with Cassady far more than the film's writers did. He was drawn to big experiences, most of which were not condoned during that era. I knew from my own story that you *could* jump into a car and leave your hometown in the rearview mirror. Of course you could, yet it's hard from today's vantage point to understand what a radical concept that was in 1950s America. Cassady lived according to his own theory that anyone can move beyond what is socially acceptable and still live an honorable life. It can be a tricky proposition, one that's fraught with unknowable consequences.

Most people pull up short of those societal boundaries. I have a thousand times, only to remember that I couldn't turn around, that forward was the only direction open to me. Neal was apolitical, as I am, and his rebellion was innate; it was simply his soul's nature. And Cassady was a trickster, unabashedly present, and therefore capable of goofing with reality as it unfolded. Naturally, I was a guy who could relate.

From the outset of the project, the producers; John Byrum; Sissy Spacek, who played Carolyn; and all of us in the cast were in agreement about taking major liberties with the particulars of Neal's life in order to get at his essence. In our story, Carolyn is in love with Neal, Jack Kerouac is in love with Neal, and Neal doesn't show much love to either of them. Jack swings from left to right, politically; Neal runs off with the hippies, goes out on the road, then comes back to Carolyn.

How true was it? Only partially. Some of our fictionalizations were forced on us by Allen Ginsberg's disdain for our project, and Carolyn's own vacillations were responsible for others. Ray Sharkey played a character named Ira, who was a fictionalized Ginsberg. We reimagined an event, for example, in which Carolyn famously caught her husband in bed with his ex-wife LuAnne and Ginsberg. In the film, it's Carolyn who's in bed with the two fellows, and we had to determine the sexual logistics. Would Carolyn lie in the middle, or—acknowledging Cassady's real-life bisexual relationship with Ginsberg—would he be in the middle, flanked by his different-gendered lovers?

When it was time to shoot the scene, I remember Sharkey asking me if I was going to play the scene nude. With my tongue very firmly in my cheek, I told him no, I wasn't, because the camera would be constantly on me and the sight of my dick would be too distracting for the audience. But I also said I recommended it. "You should try it, Ray," I continued. "I've done it. It's the most liberating thing in the world."

Ray thought about it, then decided to go for it, and I warned Byrum to prepare himself because Sharkey was determined to play the scene au naturel. The best part of my prank was seeing Ray walk out of a trailer after he'd watched the dailies of that bedroom scene. He was white as a bedsheet, mortified, just beside himself. I think he'd gotten nervous as the whole crew watched him work in the nude—and didn't appreciate how his "liberation" looked on camera.

Heart Beat was an old-fashioned-looking film when the editing was completed. Byrum used a lot of pinhole dissolves—a very dated technique where the scene ends by the frame closing in progressively to black before disappearing—and although our scenes played well, the conflicts between the characters never became real enough. I approached Cassady's ghost with my full energy, and, by and large, came up empty-handed. A few critics had glowing things to say about the interplay between me, Sissy, and John Heard as Jack—but our characters didn't do anything except move from place to place, and audiences didn't care about them. The film flopped, and I was beginning to learn by then that you can't get too attached to the success or failure of your films, you just have to move on, chuckling at the good times.

While we were shooting *Who'll Stop the Rain* in the state of Durango in Mexico, we had lots of time to create a kind of hippie heaven like the one Ken Kesey and the Merry Pranksters had built in La Honda, California. Like the Pranksters, we hung lights in the trees surrounding our compound and filled them with speakers from which we could play jammin' music all day and all night. It was wild—and everyone experimented with free love, LSD, mescaline, psilocybin, DMT, pills, pot, alcohol, beer, speed, and anything else that came our way.

One day in the middle of this, I was sitting under a tree reading former Dallas Cowboys receiver Pete Gent's novel *North Dallas Forty*. My friend and fellow actor Anthony Zerbe walked over and pointed to the book and said, "That's your next film." Anthony was a mentor and guide to me and many young actors in those days, and I was intrigued by his suggestion.

"Could I do this?" I asked incredulously.

"Absolutely!" he answered, and I believe this epiphany changed the course of my career. My acting life had allowed me to explore great writing, and now perhaps I had risen to a level where I could pursue my own material. From the moment he made that pronouncement, I knew I had to turn that terrific football novel into a movie.

When I returned to Los Angeles, I marched into International Creative Management (ICM) to have a sit-down with my agent Lou Pitt and manager Mimi Weber. I dropped a tattered copy of *North Dallas Forty* on Lou's desk and announced, "This is my next project."

Lou shook his head. "No, no, no. You can't do that. You don't own the book rights." Mimi joined in and the two of them worked me over. "Nick, you don't know how the business runs. Offers are pouring in," Mimi assured me. Lou added, "Nobody is going to be interested in *North Dallas Forty*. Let's take a look and decide your next move together." They were incredibly discouraging, and when I'd heard enough, I said, "All right, I'll see you later," and walked out the door.

I was defeated and angry, and I dropped out of sight with the phone off the hook for a while. *The Deep* had made $100 million, and I was a very hot property at the moment. Anything was possible for me, but my agent and manager were sure they knew better.

Yet instead of simply acquiescing to Mimi and Lou, I pitched the idea to Hal Hauser, a friend I'd met back in my Phoenix theater days. Hal was older than me and a successful advertising executive who had co-founded Kama Sutra, making a fortune on sensual oils and creams. He was the kind of guy who could make money easier than some people can pee, but his ambition to break into the movie business had been stymied up to that point.

Hal had bought a place not far from my ranch when Kama Sutra took off, so we got together and hatched a plan to find enough money to make the picture ourselves. We would write the screenplay together, too, we decided, and see if we could garner enough attention off of it to get one of the studios to bite.

I had agreed to help Hal dig a bass pond on his ranch for fishing, and we would begin each morning shoveling dirt out of the ground as we chatted and dug ever deeper into the story we wanted to tell. We'd hash things out for a few hours, then Hal would go inside and write while I continued to shovel. He finished the script in nine months, but bass had been swimming in his pond for four.

Early on, we agreed that it was a no-brainer to follow the story arc of the book. Its thrust and themes had the makings of a good film. Our job was to narrow the scope. Gent's narrative included a broader commentary on America at large, and a racially motivated murder was part of the plot, too. But Hal and I decided we'd stick to football, concentrating on the exploitative dynamic between ownership and coaches on one side and players on the other. Hal and I were both anti-authoritarians to our cores, so the film was destined from the outset to strongly take the players' very pissed-off point of view.

I kept a copy of Ken Kesey's *One Flew over the Cuckoo's Nest* in my back pocket like a kind of bible. *Sometimes a Great Notion,* Kesey's second and equally brilliant novel, also influenced Hal and me—both were inspired, rebellious books, and we were writing a screenplay that would make it clear that NFL football was a racist, corrupt, and dictatorial affair.

Word got out, as it always does. The phone rang and

I decided it was time to pick it up. Michael Eisner was on the other end. Eisner was a producer whom I'd first met on *Rich Man, Poor Man* when he was working for ABC, but I was so out of touch that I didn't know he had been promoted to president of Paramount Pictures. He and I would work together a fair amount in the years to come.

"What's this I hear about *North Dallas Forty?*" he inquired. I told him I'd drive our script right over, and once in Eisner's office I launched into a wholehearted sales job that went on for a good while. When I ran out of breath, Michael simply said, "I'm interested. Leave the script on my desk. I'll call tomorrow with a yes or no."

True to his word, he called the next day, telling me the script was a good one. He didn't seem at all concerned about acquiring the film rights—but he added that if we moved forward together, we would have to agree to a Paramount-appointed producer and director. I asked if I could choose among several and he assured me that I could. "Yes, we'll get you some quality film people to choose from, Nick."

That was it. We were green-lit, and the next order of business was for me to make a couple long-brewing telephone calls. I reached Lou Pitt and said, "Lou, I'm sorry, but you're fired. I just got a call from Mike

Eisner. *North Dallas Forty* is a go picture at Paramount, and you're fired." And then I called Mimi and said, "Mimi, I've just got to let you go, because you said it was impossible to do, but I've got a go picture at Paramount from Michael Eisner. I can't continue our relationship."

Mimi responded by suing me a year later. She and her lawyer wanted 10 percent of everything I would make for the rest of my film career because, she claimed, she "started" me. But the judge who finally heard our case asked me how long I had been acting before I met Mimi, to which I replied about fifteen years.

"How many plays did you do in that time?"

"About two hundred fifty," I replied.

"Well, that's quite a rep," he said, then asked, "Have you done movies, too?"

"Yes, Your Honor, here and there," I said, and that was all the judge wanted to know before telling Mimi, "I just can't see you getting part of this man's salary for the rest of his life. He has paid you fifteen percent of each deal in which you've represented him, and that's all I believe you are fairly owed."

Mimi worked at ICM, and its head, Jeff Berg, had called me again and again in the days following my firing of Mimi. When I finally took his call, Jeff said, "Look, Nick, we know we fucked up, no question about it, we fucked up. But, let me tell you, we can do great things for you, we really can. This will never happen to you again. Will you come in and talk to us?"

I thought about it for a moment, then gave him one condition. "Okay. I'll come in if you'll have one of your agents meet me in the parking lot with a longneck bottle of beer."

We made a deal, and sure enough, a guy met me with a bottle of beer, which I drank on the way up to Jeff's office.

He was ready for me, telling me once again that ICM had really fucked up, assuring me that it would never happen again, and adding that the company had just the agent who could handle me brilliantly, and who would doggedly pursue the ideas I had and the movies in which I wanted to star.

Then Sue Mengers walked in, and I certainly knew who Sue was, although I'd never met her. She was big. She represented people like Candice Bergen, Michael Caine, Cher, Gene Hackman, Sidney Lumet, Steve McQueen, Ryan O'Neal, Burt Reynolds, Barbra Streisand, and many others, and now she wanted to take me on. "Honey," she quickly told me, "I'm so sorry you went through that shit. Of course, I will pursue everything that you're interested in from here on out. And what's more, I'll *get* it for you."

Sue's assurance—and that beer that had been waiting in the parking lot—were all I needed. I remained
at ICM and Sue became my agent, and we worked together wonderfully for a long time.

Making *North Dallas Forty* over the next year was
both a nightmare and a dream. In my experience,
sometimes these things are either luck or karma, and
other times you must *make* change happen—remaining
true to your own instincts, taking your own advice, and
forging ahead to achieve what you believe is important.

I knew what a brutal business football can be—both
on and off the field. And by now I could see parallels
between how ball players and actors were often treated
by people whose power over them could profoundly
limit their options and sometimes even wreck their
lives. I couldn't help but believe that one of my life's
important undertakings was going to be getting *North
Dallas Forty* to the screen—who better than me, after
all?—and somehow, I was pulling it off. Paramount had
committed to the movie, I would choose both the producer and the director, and the legendary Sue Mengers
was now by my side. I felt like I had just scored on a
ninety-nine-yard run from scrimmage.

I would play Phil Elliott in *North Dallas Forty,* a
character largely based on Pete Gent himself. As

producer, I chose Frank Yablans—a guy who was as tough a motherfucker as they come. Yablans had been Paramount's president until he'd tried to throw the studio's owner, Charlie Bluhdorn, out a window one day when the two had encountered what you could call a substantive disagreement. Frank fired away at me from the get-go, declaring, "I'll be the goddamned owner of the franchise! I don't give a fuck!" For a split second, I thought he was auditioning for the role of the team owner in the film, but then I caught his drift. Frank didn't care who he had to run over. Whatever it took, he was going to get the picture made.

Ted Kotcheff was the director I selected from among those Paramount offered for the project. I had seen his film *The Apprenticeship of Duddy Kravitz,* with Richard Dreyfuss, which had won the Golden Bear at the 1974 Berlin Film Festival. It's an excellent picture, and I was already comfortable with the idea that Ted would direct us, but he won me over entirely when we first met and he confessed, "Nick, I don't know anything about football." That was exactly what I wanted to hear, and I told him the movie was much more about fighting corrupt institutions—*any* institution—than it was a sports film, and he had proven his chops as a dramatist a number of times over. What I didn't immediately tell him was that he was taking on an impossible job—not simply directing the picture, but also attempting to find some common ground between Yablans and the rest of us.

During the development process, we had gone through lots of writers, including one who was convinced that *North Dallas Forty* was properly a slapstick comedy, complete with a player who sported a wooden leg. I grew worried that we could lose the very essence of our film, so I called Pete Gent and asked him to come join us on the set, which made Frank Yablans crazy. "Get this guy the hell off our set!" he screamed.

I explained to Frank that this was the man who wrote the novel. This *was* Phil Elliott, the character I was playing. I needed him. We all did.

Frank grumbled and acquiesced, and Ted got Pete busy rewriting the script. Frank wasn't on set the first time we shot one of Pete's rewritten scenes, and when he later saw it in dailies, he came up to us and announced that it was brilliant. "Who wrote this?" he demanded.

When Pete humbly raised his hand, Frank barked back, "Well, keep writing, goddamn it!" But there was never any love lost between the two men as we continued to shoot. One time, in fact, Pete became so frustrated by Frank's changing demands that he picked him up by the lapels, apparently determined to throw him for a touchdown. But then he thought better of the idea, and set Yablans down and began to cry with frustration. His decision not to go absolutely postal only resulted in Yablans's taunting him. "You've got no guts, Gent. You didn't have the guts to kill me. That's the difference between us. I'd have killed you!" It would have been the most dramatic scene in the movie if we had filmed it.

Even though we were shooting Pete Gent's own fictionalized story, I felt I really needed more consultative input from an NFL player—and a wide receiver specifically—than Pete alone could offer. As I initially read the novel, I kept imagining the legendary Oakland Raiders receiver Fred Biletnikoff as Phil Elliott physically. Biletnikoff wasn't big or fast by NFL standards. Instead he used guile, guts, and a remarkable pair of hands to overachieve his way into the Hall of Fame. He was a student and great practitioner of the game. When I reached out to Fred, we talked about the correlations between the art of film and the art of sports, and once he was convinced of my commitment to excellence, he agreed to become a consultant.

Fred looked much more like a chain-smoking used-car salesman than your usual image of a football player. Yet he was a well-grounded, detail-oriented, nuts-and-bolts workaholic. But he could be a little far-out, too. "Don't carry the route in your head because a cornerback can read your mind," he coached me. "Forget where you're going until you get there. Improvise precisely." His understanding of the wide receiver position was extraordinary, and I took every cue from him I possibly could as I created the film version of Phil Elliott.

Fred didn't wear knee pads and so neither did Phil. Fred yanked the middle flaps out of his shoulder pads to increase his chances of making overhead catches, and so did Phil. I made sure that Phil taped his arms up precisely like Fred did before each game. And on-screen I also imitated Fred's final act of preparation before every game, lying on his back and meditatively tossing a football toward the ceiling. Fred coached me through every scene we shot, and the film wouldn't have been the same—or nearly as good—without him.

The NFL did its best to torpedo the film once its administrators got word that we were in production. They hated the idea that we might tarnish their image if we demonstrated what second-class citizens its players were—regardless of their race—and how terribly crippled almost every veteran became. It was a wild ride, but with Pete's great story, Fred's inspired consulting, and wonderful performances from actors like Mac Davis, the country singing sensation who made his on-screen debut in the film, I felt confident we were creating something special. Mac played Seth Maxwell, a character based closely on the colorful Dallas Cowboys quarterback Don Meredith, and Mac simply sparkled on camera.

He couldn't throw a football to save his life, but we were just making a movie, after all; Mac only had to pretend he was a quarterback, and I was happy reviewers gave him glowing notices when the film premiered. You can imagine how sweet it felt when the film was a financial success and a critical one as well. It was *my* film; I'd fought for it and bled for it and given it my all. I'll never forget the afternoon when Sue Mengers pushed a *New York Times* review of *North Dallas Forty* under my nose. "The uncontested star of the show is Mr. Nolte," it read, "who may surprise a lot of people who had the ill fortune to see him in *The Deep* and the even worse luck to miss him in *Who'll Stop the Rain*. His performance in *Who'll Stop the Rain* was altogether stunning; this time out he's engaging and full of surprises. Either way, he's something to see."

In the seventies and eighties, there was a bar at the corner of the Pacific Coast Highway and Trancas Canyon Road. It was a local hangout, legendary for hard partying and unannounced, off-the-cuff rock shows.

Fleetwood Mac, the Stones, and other world-famous acts would appear out of the blue, plug in, and tear it up. You never knew when it would happen, but when it did, the place went nuts. On a quiet night in 1980, I met the actor and playwright Jason Miller there. A black-Irishman from Scranton, Pennsylvania, he had written a Pulitzer Prize–winning play called *That Championship Season* about a reunion of high school basketball teammates.

After Jason and I talked at length at the bar, getting more than a little slaughtered, we continued to his house, where he showed me his screenplay based on the play. It was about to become a film directed by William Friedkin, who had won an Academy Award for directing *The French Connection* a few years before. Jason then asked me, was I interested?

Damn right I was. Martin Sheen and Paul Sorvino were already attached to play team members, and George C. Scott was on board to play the coach. Friedkin himself was a basketball junkie in addition to being one of the nation's finest directors, so I couldn't see how the film could go wrong. But then, a couple of weeks before shooting was set to begin, I got a call from George C. Scott while Legs and I were staying at Caesars in Lake Tahoe with our friend Don Johnson and Amarillo Slim, the notorious gambler.

"There was a fight. I wasn't drunk. This guy Fried-kin is a nut. He's crazy. I've already lost one testicle in this business, I'm not going to lose another," Scott shouted.

Scott and Friedkin had gotten embroiled in an argument at a party at Martin Sheen's. Ugly words had been spoken. Serious threats had been made, and Scott swore he would walk if Friedkin continued as the picture's director.

The situation was clearly quite serious, so I left Legs to continue her partying—pulling her away from a good time was like separating a lion from fresh meat—and I flew back to Southern California, where I found Jason at his house in Malibu, halfway into a bottle of whiskey and shouting, "It's over! It's over!"

But it wasn't, of course. I helped Jason with his whiskey and convinced him we were just getting started, and the two of us determined over several hours that it was up to us to come up with a new plan. We knew we couldn't replace Billy Friedkin. Directors are less selfish and a little more human than actors. They hold themselves with a certain decorum, making them less likely to eat their own. No director worth a goddamn would take the job if Friedkin was out, so another coach was the answer. We bandied names around, and finally,

Jason suggested William Holden. Perfect, I said, and I promised I would go get him.

With the help of Sue Mengers, I was able to reach Holden by phone, capture his interest, and secure his promise to read the script. A week later, he met Jason at a bar, where the two shared several drinks and Holden offered the news that he loved the script and would accept the role. Next, we tracked down Billy Friedkin in Europe, he immediately approved Holden as the coach, and we finally appeared to be all set.

A new shooting schedule was created and start date was chosen, and everything was lining up nicely a few weeks later when Jason, deeply depressed, informed me that Stefanie Powers had recently dumped Holden while he was in Africa, and his boozing had gotten so out of control that none of his buddies would drink with him anymore; even Glenn Ford's wife wouldn't let Glenn drink with Bill anymore.

"Well, shit," I replied, "all we have to do is find him and drink with him, set him straight, and get him ready to shoot." But we couldn't find him. We tried his house, his bar, his friends' houses and friends' bars. We even tried to find him in Africa, but we couldn't.

After coming up empty for three days, I was fried. I went home. The next morning, I was in bed asleep when Jason came in and shook me awake, saying, "Did you hear? Did you hear? Bill Holden is dead." He'd been alone and drunk and had fallen, hitting his head on a coffee table and bleeding to death in his living room. The police told us they counted twenty-eight messages on his answering machine, which were left by Jason and me as his body waited for days to be discovered.

It was a crushing blow. That was it; there would be no *Championship Season* for me. I was spooked. I wanted *nothing* more to do with that picture, regardless of the quality of the story, the writing, or the cast. I bailed, and then so did Billy Friedkin. Jason finally directed the movie himself, replacing me with Bruce Dern, and he made a good picture in the end.

Coming down off a successful film takes me a month or more, and always has. But getting over a sad fiasco like that one seemed impossible, and I didn't know how to move beyond it. I found a rental house near Point Dume in Malibu, where only Legs and a couple of other people knew I was hiding out. I took the phone off the hook, I didn't venture out, and I drank, snorted coke, and sank into my biggest depression in many years.

Only five years had passed since I'd portrayed Tom Jordache to great acclaim in *Rich Man, Poor Man,* and my career had then taken a meteoric rise. I'd gotten remarkably good reviews in three more theatrical films in the intervening years, and I had brought one of those stories to the screen with only my own tenacity. I'd met a wild woman I adored, one who shared my rebellious streak. We had married and were living full tilt. How could this forty-year-old imagine a better half decade than the one he'd just had?

Yet there I was again—stymied by real life, laid low by the kinds of challenges that come everyone's way. I hid for weeks inside that house perched on the edge of paradise, wishing that I could always live my life inside a script.

Chapter 10
Under Fire

The funk into which I fell after *That Championship Season* didn't disappear until my friend Dino Conti knocked on my door. I'd known Dino for a long time—it was Dino who had whispered a few words into Legs's ear on the evening I met her—and I always enjoyed his company. Sure, everybody said that Dino was mob connected, and that seemed like a likely enough possibility, but I didn't care.

I'd met him through another Dino—Dino De Laurentiis, a self-made movie mogul from Italy who had relocated to the U.S. and shaken up the industry with a series of films that included *Serpico, Death Wish, Ragtime, Conan the Barbarian, Blue Velvet,* and many others. Tiny in stature and always larger than life, Dino was one of the most prolific producers in the history of film. He made pictures of every kind and made them with panache. The fact that people could never figure out where his money came from added an air of intrigue to him and his operation. They don't make them like him anymore, and I was drawn to him as soon as I met him.

He had originally hired Dino Conti to protect his children following a death threat, but the two Dinos clearly had more than their Italian roots in common and spent lots of time together. Dino De Laurentiis began to pitch a steady stream of projects to me early in my career, and every time we met, Dino the bodyguard, Dino the reputed mob guy, was with him.

Our regular meetings were fantastic—always a blast—if seldom fruitful for either of us. He was set to produce a lavish remake of *The Great Train Robbery* for a while, and it was a film I really wanted a piece of. He'd assure me in his heavy accent, "Of course, you'll do *Train Robbery*, but first you do *Orca*." But I wouldn't have it. I'd hold my ground and answer, "No, Dino, I'm not going to do *Orca*. Just forget it." Round and round we went like that for years, and when De Laurentiis would throw up his arms in frustration, I'd look over at Dino Conti, who was always present, and say, "Dino, let's grab a bite to eat."

Conti walked me out of the office every time, and

when we hit the sidewalk, the first thing he would do was stroll over to the FBI guys permanently parked outside his boss De Laurentiis's office to say hello. It always made me nervous, and I'd implore him not to mess with those guys, but he assured me that it was clean fun. We shared many lunches and I always had a good time. I'm a talker, and Conti was a good listener. But his boss never understood why I liked hanging out with him as much as I did. He'd repeatedly ask, "Why you like this guy? You know what he does?"

I knew; I just didn't want to know too much, and Conti wasn't about to offer me details in any case. There was just something about him that made me want to say yes to virtually anything he suggested. So I knew I was in trouble the moment I saw Conti standing in the doorway at the house in Point Dume. "Come on, Nick," he announced. "Enough of this laying around. Let's go play with the boys."

I didn't know what that meant, yet Conti wouldn't take no for an answer and I finally relented, although I complained the entire length of the drive down the PCH into the city. When we reached Paramount Studios, Dino was clearly a man with a plan, and he marched me into an executive office where I was welcomed with big smiles by producers Michael Eisner, Larry Gordon, and Don Simpson; two coffee boys who would become high-powered executives them-selves, Jeffrey Katzenberg and Joel Silver; and director Walter Hill, who had recently had great success with films like *Hard Times, The Driver,* and *The Long Riders.*

I may have still been in a deep hole of depression, but as Dino slid over to their side, it didn't take me more than a second to recognize that this was a setup; they had recruited him to bring me in. Walter dove into his pitch, telling me that he wanted me to read a script. "It's the worst script you'll ever read," Walter told me. "But take it home and get back to me in a couple of days." When I asked why in the hell he was pitching me a terrible screenplay, he was nonchalant. "We just thought you should know where we're starting from. I'm going to rewrite it and I'm going to make it, and we all want you to star in it."

When Walter and I talked again, I agreed that the story was shit. It was about two white cops in San Francisco, and absolutely nothing happened. I was curious why Walter had wasted my time, but he was unperturbed. I had said no to many pictures by then, but somehow, I couldn't this time, and I was able to get Walter and Paramount to agree to send me up to San Francisco to nose around for a bit and see if I could dig up a storyline, an angle, a character—*something* that might redeem this piece of crap that Walter and company appeared so determined to make.

Soon thereafter I headed north with my friend and assistant at the time, Billy Cross, an Oklahoma-raised Vietnam vet who had found his way to the fringes of Hollywood. Billy and I had drinks with a detective Paramount had selected for us to meet, and he, in turn, put us in touch with just the guy we needed, a black detective who agreed to show us the city's criminal underbelly for a few days if we promised never to reveal his identity. Toward the end of the second day, the guy made our trip worthwhile and set history in motion.

When he *really* needed information, he explained, he would go to the city jail and look for a promising candidate, a current inmate whose rap sheet and known associates seemed perfect for the task at hand, then would check him out of the slammer for exactly forty-eight hours. The two men would spend time scouring certain neighborhoods, where the inmate-turned-snitch would identify crooks and their specialties, methods, and chain of command. With the wealth of new information, the detective would pressure small-timers identified by the guy on loan to turn on bigger fish, who then would decide to squeal themselves rather than go to jail, and before long the detective had made his case—or several.

It was gold—absolute gold—and for the first time I thought we might find a way to make the movie. Walter was thrilled. "Fantastic! There's my hook!" he proclaimed as he dove into his rewrite. And as he locked himself into a room for a couple of weeks, I agreed to his request to go to New York to meet a black comedian from *Saturday Night Live* who Walter thought might be perfect to play the con whom my character would escort around the city for forty-eight hours.

I wasn't a fan of *Saturday Night Live*. The very few times I'd watched it in its earliest days, I picked up a faux-sixties vibe that rubbed me the wrong way. I had no idea who was currently part of the cast, and I'd never heard of Eddie Murphy, the young and reputedly hypertalented comedian Walter wanted me to meet. After I reached New York, I hooked up with a black saxophone player I had made friends with many years earlier, and we quickly loaded up on coke and binged hard for old times' sake.

A couple of days in, I mentioned that I was in town to meet the black guy from *Saturday Night Live* about the possibility of starring in a movie together. But my old friend was immediately quite concerned. "You can't use him, Nick," he said gravely. "He's a base-head."

I enjoyed our partying for the rest of the week, then returned to Los Angeles, where I shared the bad news with Walter in his office, telling him matter-of-factly that we couldn't hire Eddie Murphy for the role because he was a base-head. Walter saw right through me. "Eddie Murphy? A base-head? You didn't meet him, did you, Nick?"

I folded, admitting that I hadn't actually *met* Eddie, no, but nonetheless I had learned of his addiction from a very reliable source. I tried to make a joke so we could simply laugh the whole thing off, but Walter wasn't amused. "That's the last time I'll send you out to do anything," he assured me, and all I could do was acquiesce to his choice. "Just cast him, man," I said, surrendering. "It'll work out."

The saxophone player had presumed that I meant Garrett Morris, the original *SNL* cast member who had left the show in 1980. Eddie Murphy, on the other hand, I quickly discovered, was a twenty-year-old comic "genius" from Brooklyn who had taken his first season on *Saturday Night Live* by storm and who, people predicted, was poised to have a huge career in television and in film.

I was already settled into the San Francisco hotel where we would be staying during the shoot for the film that now was titled *48 Hrs.* when Eddie arrived. I made a point of meeting him in the hotel lobby and invited him to my room, where I introduced him to my assistant Billy Cross and showed him the Pac-Man and Space Invaders video games I'd had installed in my room, and Eddie—still just a kid—was *impressed*.

"Can I get an assistant?" he wanted to know, and I told him sure. "Can I get some arcade games, too?" Yes, I said, nodding, he could. "Just call the producers when you need something and tell them what it is and, yeah, they'll get it for you," I said, and Eddie was amazed, thinking it sounded like making movies was going to be a real workable deal for him.

48 Hrs. was going to be an action-comedy featuring two unlikely partners—and none of us had a clue that its success would spawn a whole "buddy cop" subgenre that would include *Beverly Hills Cop, Lethal Weapon,* and *Rush Hour.* All we knew at the time we shot it was that we had a great concept, a workable script, and two leads who were proving to have great chemistry together in the dailies despite the fact that Eddie and I came from very different backgrounds and that I was twenty years older than him.

I played plenty of pranks on Eddie and he, in turn, constantly assaulted me with his quick wit and sharp tongue. His astonishing ability to ad-lib in very funny ways improved the movie virtually every day.

Eddie and I regularly threw racial slurs at each other

and flashed anger in our scenes, raising the eyebrows of lots of people in the process. By the early 1980s, only *Lilies of the Field* and *In the Heat of the Night* had dared to let whites and blacks yell at each other on-screen, and the nation was still in the midst of a long and awkward effort on the part of both groups to find comfortable ways in which to communicate. Could a white guy call a black guy a "brother"? Could a black guy tell a white dude he was full of shit? No one—least of all the filmmakers—was sure of what the post-civil-rights-movement rules were.

I tried to get Eddie to call me "Banana Skin," because that was the affectionate name the black musicians in Omaha's jazz clubs had called me when I was a teenage kid, but Eddie wanted no part of it. "What's that even mean?" he asked. "That's just weird, motherfucker. I'm not going to call you no 'Banana Skin.'" There was a fundamental element of each of us that was nonracial, and it allowed us to really develop our unique relationship in the film. Yes, the white guy was the cop and the black guy was the criminal, but Eddie's character Reggie was much more sophisticated and smarter in many ways.

Eddie had a background in boxing, and he lobbied for his character Reggie to be an Olympic boxing champion—something that was fine with me. But when

Eddie suggested that the two of us should truly box on camera, I just had to mess with him. "Oh, fuck, Eddie, you wouldn't get a punch on me. Seriously. If you try, I'll knock you clean through the wall." Instead of boxing, in the end, we focused on the two characters' hugely unpredictable volatility, as well as creating comic action of every kind—plus a hell of a lot of gunplay.

Eddie was more than a little skittish about guns, but I helped him get comfortable. I taught him the two-handed revolver grip that I'd learned from cops at the Los Angeles Police Department; it was real, and it looked dramatic as hell, and I couldn't help but notice how it later became virtually the only way an actor would shoot a handgun on film in the years to follow.

Walter Hill was great about letting me do the driving of the old Cadillac ragtop that we careened around the city in. I would have hated to have a double do the driving, but I didn't have to worry, as it turned out. Walter had a camera mounted on the hood of the car and let me have at it, and I just kind of went wild behind the wheel—narrowly avoiding serious accidents a few times and regularly scaring the shit out of Eddie.

When the film was released in December 1982, it was an immediate hit and went on to earn $80 million in domestic box-office receipts alone. Although no one took the movie too seriously—we didn't intend for them to, after all—it continued to raise my film profile ever higher, and Eddie even received a Golden Globe nomination for best male film debut of the year a few months following the film's release. He went on to have a great run as a comedic actor, but he and I ultimately looked at our careers a bit differently.

He telephoned after *48 Hrs.* had become a bona fide hit, asking for advice. Paramount was offering him $120 million for seven pictures and he wanted to know what I thought. I hesitated for a minute, then said, "Listen, man, I'm not going to tell you to turn down a hundred and twenty million dollars, but if you make a deal like that, you get roped to Paramount. You may get a good script the first time, then maybe another one, but the rest—who knows? They usually run out of creativity. But if you stay independent and go to this studio, then to that one, you can probably bid your price up and get even more money."

He listened, but Eddie decided to take the offer. Some time later, he told me he wanted to be doing what I was doing—artistically satisfying, small, gritty movies. I told him he ought to, but warned that he'd have to cut his salary.

"Oh, I can't do that, Nick," Eddie responded, as if I'd just said he'd have to cut off his hand. "I have my needs, man."

The suits at Paramount had believed early on that they had a real hit on their hands with *48 Hrs.* They were so bullish on its prospects, in fact, that they let it sit in the can for most of a year so it could be a Christmas-season release. Those kinds of decisions are entirely out of an actor's hands—unless you're both starring and producing, of course, which I virtually never was. Delaying the movie only meant that I would make another movie following the *48 Hrs.* shoot, and it would be released ten months before *48 Hrs.;* that happened several times over the years.

I'd been surprised to discover that literary people back east looked down their noses a bit at the work of John Steinbeck, his Nobel Prize notwithstanding. I loved his books—not so much the big, heavy Depression-era books, but the simpler, more sympathetic comic novels like *Sweet Thursday* and *Cannery Row,* as well as his hugely popular memoir *Travels with Charley.*

I knew David Ward, who had won an Academy Award for his screenplay for *The Sting* a decade earlier, had written a screen adaptation of *Cannery Row* and *Sweet Thursday,* and I liked it a lot and thought David understood the material well enough to direct the picture, which would be his first. The script was languishing at Orion and its prospects for ever getting

made weren't good, but I told Sue Mengers that Steinbeck was a giant in need of exploring, and I added that
David Ward's idea to shoot the entire film on a soundstage was a terrific one. It would look and feel a bit like
a play and that was something that would support the
material's literary qualities, I was sure.

Indomitable Sue went to bat for me once more;
this time she called David Begelman, the new head of
MGM. Begelman had survived a very messy 1977 em-
bezzlement scandal at Columbia Pictures—even after
being convicted, fined, and forced to do community
service. Sue painted a pretty picture for him. "Look,
David," she told him. "This is your first year at MGM.
You need to establish yourself as an executive who
makes twenty films this next year. You need to have
good strong commercial films in there. And you've got
to have prestigious literature in there, too. And I've got
the literary piece. It's *Cannery Row,* and it will star
Nick Nolte as Doc Ricketts, and we'll find the woman."

Sue was legendarily persuasive, and David said yes.
But he changed his mind not long after we'd signed
contracts. I think his ego kicked in and he didn't want
to restart his career with a movie that he had been
cajoled into doing. "Nick, I'll pay you your full two
million," he said when he telephoned, "but let's just
call it a day."

I told him we *had* to make the movie, and I per-
severed, even as Begelman continued to sabotage the
picture. "I'm going to make it real tough in casting,"
he later warned. "You don't have any choice. Raquel
Welch or Liza Minnelli for the part of Suzy." I thought
both were completely wrong as Doc Ricketts's girlfriend. I held fast.

"David," I told him, "I don't care if you hire Maude
fucking Frickert, I'm going to *make* this film."

True to his word, David did cast Raquel in the role
of Suzy, although she, too, thought she was too old for
the part. I told her, "Rocket, just show up on time.
It'll be fine." Rocket was my affectionate name for
her. She took my advice to heart and showed up at the
soundstage already wearing her makeup long before
her call every morning. But Begelman, the son of a
bitch, fired her for being late nonetheless. He sued her
in an attempt to get back the money she'd been paid,
and Rocket sued MGM in return, claiming the studio
was trying to ruin her career by telling the world that
she was difficult to work with. It would be six years
before a jury awarded her $10 million in damages for
being wrongly fired, and Begelman's career spiraled
downward until he committed suicide in 1995.

In the very early 1980s, however, David Begelman

was still a very powerful and influential man, and I was determined not to let him have his way and kill what I believed could be a good picture. David Ward and I knew that the first order of business was to keep shooting every scene in the picture that didn't require Suzy, which would give us a couple more weeks of work and ensure that, by then, Begelman's financial commitment would be so big that he simply couldn't fold up the tent. I told Ward that I knew that our Suzy would find us in time.

The set our crew had constructed was magnificent—so big that it encompassed two soundstages—and it was an uncanny replication of what the real Cannery Row in Monterey looked like in photographs and paintings from the 1930s and 1940s. Word got around so widely that our set was something special that industry people like Elizabeth Taylor and John Huston visited just to see it for themselves. I loved its feel. You got the sense that the set was real and make-believe at the same time—and to help me pour as much of myself into my character Doc as I could, I began to sleep on the set, on the same cot where Doc slept amidst his menagerie of sea animals. It was so groovy; at night the octopi would crawl out of their tanks and make their way across the floor to find crackers and crumbs lying around. It became second nature for me to scoop them up and get them back into their tanks before the cast and crew arrived each morning.

One day, as I was sitting on the steps outside Doc's place, a girl walked by and bumped my chair with a laugh. "And who are you?" I asked.

"Oh, I'm just here to see the set," she said.

"You're Suzy, aren't you?" I asked her.

She smiled coyly at me before she replied, "I don't know. Who's Suzy?"

I hadn't seen the recent megahit *Urban Cowboy,* so I didn't know who Debra Winger was, but I was immediately curious about this young woman who was checking us out. And it didn't take long for Ward, me, and everyone to learn that Debra's agent knew we needed an actress and had urged her to stop by and see whether she might be keen on becoming my love interest, Suzy.

Debra was beautiful, in her own way, and she had a wicked sense of humor that I really loved. She had a reputation for being rough and constantly demanding to be the center of attention, but we *needed* our Suzy— needed her *now*—so we offered Debra the part and she accepted it before she left that afternoon. She would be utterly believable as one of the *Cannery* girls, I knew, but I wouldn't know until a day or two later that she could also be hellfire to work with.

One evening a couple of weeks into what I began calling "The Debra Show," David Ward invited me to join him, his brother, and Debra for spaghetti at a nearby restaurant. Our food arrived as Debra was regaling us with jokes, imitating my gravelly voice, and generally holding court. I noticed her give David a kind of "say it" look before he turned to me and announced out of the blue, "You know, Nick, I've never worked with a more unprofessional actor. You've been very difficult to work with."

He continued his rant and I looked puzzled, I'm sure. I looked at his brother, but his brother simply looked the other way. When I turned to see what Debra was making of David's little tirade, she was grinning like a Cheshire cat. She clearly had pressed David to give me some shit, and he was doing it simply because she had wrapped him around her finger. I wasn't happy, not a bit, but instead of saying something harsh to David, I scooped up my spaghetti in both palms and smashed it into my face. I rubbed it in real good for a second or two, then picked up my hat and walked away.

The next day, Debra gushed to me that what I'd done was the coolest thing she'd ever seen. And sure enough, it wasn't long before Debra, too, was smashing food into her face in public. In something of the same vein, it wasn't rare for her to come into my trailer in the morning and say hello and then, wham, hit me. Yet much of her erratic behavior, we assumed, was caused by her constant worry about her father, who she said had suffered a massive heart attack and was only clinging to life by a thread.

That seemed to explain a great deal and Debra got away with all kinds of capricious behavior because of her family crisis. The picture really suffered due to her antics and the way they affected everyone on both sides of the camera, and it wasn't surprising that Debra thought it was just funny as hell when she invited her father—whose health had been fine all along—to join her at the wrap party when our shoot was finished.

All I knew was that I was *very* happy to be moving on. She had toyed with virtually everyone on the set in her quest for her own kind of control, and it wasn't any surprise that audiences and critics responded to the film as a very mixed bag. I got generally good notices—and Debra did, too—but it wasn't the film I had poured my heart into early on, and I was learning that that was often simply the way things went.

Cannery Row was a film with a fine young director and a brilliant art director, and it was the first U.S. film by Sven Nykvist, the legendary Swedish cinematographer who shot Ingmar Bergman's films. The set was magical, as I've mentioned; the story was Steinbeck at his best; and our cast—Debra included—was comprised of strong actors. But the film, in the end, was a picture that was much less than the sum of its parts.

Sometimes a film's many elements simply don't come together as they might have. Other times—and it occurred with my next film, *Under Fire*—everything goes wrong during the shoot and even getting the picture completed looks like a hell of a long shot, but somehow the finished film is brilliant by the time it reaches theaters. It's my opinion that *Under Fire* is an overlooked gem.

I didn't know about the chaos under way in Nicaragua until I chanced on Roger Spottiswoode, who had written *48 Hrs.*, and screenwriter Ron Shelton in the commissary at Paramount one day, where they were about to pitch the *Under Fire* script, which they had cowritten. I expressed interest in the project, which they said was about journalists caught in the midst of a Central American revolution, and when I read it I was blown away. I wanted in, wanted to play Russell Price, an apolitical news photographer who falls for a radio journalist in war-ravaged Nicaragua, and both Roger and Ron were happy to attach me to the project and get my support.

Sue Mengers was able to wrangle about $7 million in financing; we found $5 million more, and just as we arrived in the Mexican states of Chiapas and Oaxaca to shoot, the peso was devalued by half, so we had effectively $24 million with which to make something epic in scope.

As the story unfolds, it doesn't take my character Russell long to see the vast difference between the corrupt, U.S.-backed dictatorship and the struggling guerrilla forces who have been fighting for their independence for a decade already. As his eyes are opened, he and Claire, who was played by Joanna Cassidy, decide to go along with the rebels and film their fighting behind the lines. During one battle, a much-venerated rebel leader is shot dead, and Russell reluctantly agrees to fake a photo of the man as though he were still living to boost the spirits of the rebels. The photo appears in the news around the world, and the idea that the leader could still be alive causes such a furor that Claire's lover, Alex, a television newsman, thinking the leader is alive as well, shows up to interview him for American TV. It's on the way to the interview that Alex leaves the car for a moment and is senselessly shot and killed by a government soldier, the whole episode filmed for the world by Russell.

It's a powerful story, and it was very topical at the

time we shot it—by then Nicaragua had spiraled from civil war to revolution—but the Mexico shoot was like a revolution itself much of the time. The string of catastrophes began when we accidentally blew up a Mexican citizen's car in Oaxaca, and the local press referred to us as "Under Fire Under Assholes." Then, I was at dinner one night with a Mexican guy who was supplying me with a little local blow, and he became indignant that I didn't speak any Spanish, even though our little business relationship was working pretty well for him. "Why do you not learn Spanish?" he asked as he ominously grabbed me by the cheek. "You come down here a lot but you don't learn nothing." I apologized, promised him I would try to learn Spanish, then successfully freed my cheek from his fingers. It was spooky.

At that same dinner, other locals came up and expressed outrage that the production hadn't paid the city a fee to shoot there. We had paid the governor of Oaxaca, I explained, but paying him off was something entirely different from paying the officials of the city, I quickly learned. Then three thousand indigenous people—who each had been promised fifteen dollars a day to work as "revolution" extras—mutinied when there was only enough budgeted to pay fifteen hundred of them. I intervened by pulling a local aside and advising him to have them sit down all around our vehicles on set and refuse to move until the producers found the money. It worked; they apologized profusely and paid those poor people, and we were rolling again. The suits may have an entirely different version of this event, but I'm sticking to mine.

Joanna Cassidy, who played Claire, the love interest of both my character Russell and Alex, the newsman played by Gene Hackman, treated us both a bit like we had leprosy throughout the shoot, and neither one of us understood why until someone explained that she was dating the very married British director Ridley Scott. Ridley—knowing how quickly on-set romances could catch fire—had instructed her to stay the hell away and not give either of us a glimmer of hope for shenanigans with her, and Joanna was strictly obeying.

Then our cast and crew of about eighty people flew south to Tuxtla Gutiérrez in Chiapas. We had eighty crew members on the plane. I was sitting with a Mexican stuntman, Tarzan, who was kind of a charismatic, fun guy, and the dolly grip, Apache. I was with the Mexican crew because I just found them more comfortable. As we came in to Tuxtla, it was heavily fogged and we were in the cloud bank. The airport runway was at a very high altitude and the pilot was trying to find the landing strip. I was looking out the window and I couldn't see the ground, or anything, really. It was terrifying, and the pilot decided to pull up and fly back to Oaxaca.

That sudden change in plans outraged director Roger Spottiswoode and his lapdog assistant director enough that they stormed the cockpit, screaming, "Land us! Land us right now, you Mexican motherfuckers!"

But many others on board, me among them, had absolutely no interest in dying that day and we were delighted when our fine cinematographer, John Alcott, and his gaffer jumped Spottiswoode and his AD and pinned them down long enough for the pilots to get their door safely locked and continue us on toward Oaxaca.

In the scuffle that continued, terror and tempers flared even further; Tarzan and Apache got into the action and things were real Western when we landed back in Oaxaca. Once back in the lobby, we heard an overhead announcement: "The following people will not be allowed in Mexican airspace on any plane, private or commercial: Roger Spottiswoode, Nick Nolte . . . ," and a list of everyone on the crew. I said, "There you go, boys, deal with that. I hear there is not even a road to Tuxtla." We were screwed.

Well, there was a road, but it could barely be called that. What it turned out to be was a seventeen-hour taxi ride over jeep roads and two-track trails to get south to Chiapas. I was out of pain pills, out of all my stashes, and I was sure, at times, that I wasn't going to make it. When we finally arrived, we just had a couple of action scenes remaining to shoot, but sure enough, things turned once again into chaos. We succeeded in destroying a thousand-year-old cemetery with tanks we had rented from the Mexican army, and for that, we were informed, everything of any value we possessed was going to be confiscated by the national government—our final rolls of exposed film included.

Mike Medavoy, the chairman of Orion Pictures, had received word back in Los Angeles about the planned confiscations and had reached me at my hotel in Tuxtla to give me precise instructions. He evidently couldn't trust Spottiswoode to safely get the film out of the country, but he did trust me. On the last day of shooting, we would be out in boats on nearby Lago Malpaso, filming the final day of the revolution as my character and Joanna's character flee by water with victorious Sandinista soldiers in tow.

Late in the afternoon, as Spottiswoode was filming from shore, I did precisely as Mike had requested, telling the boat's driver to turn us around and get us back to camp as fast as the boat could travel. From the shore, Spottiswoode screamed, "Where are you going? Stop!

Stop!" from a bullhorn. The boat's driver looked at me nervously but I motioned him forward and we pressed on. At that point, a worried Joanna said to me, "You know, Nick, I have not been a really warm compatriot on this shoot. I was not very warm with Gene either; I am sorry for that. But you obviously know something is about to go down. Could I go with you?" I said, "Sure, Joanna."

When we finally reached the shore, we jumped into a waiting cab, sped to Joanna's trailer so she could grab some essentials, then went on to the Tuxtla airport, where John Alcott's gaffer was waiting with the last rolls of film, along with a plane Medavoy had sent from L.A.

Joanna and I jumped on board—ignoring the immigration officials who were pissed off about what we gringos were up to—and we safely flew west out of Mexican airspace, then northwest to LAX and a wild end to the roughest shoot I'd ever been part of.

Mike Medavoy had already become a legend in the international film community by the time he saved the day and got the final essential images of *Under Fire* safely out of Mexico, escorted by Joanna and me. I was grateful for his leadership and his friendship—especially after learning once we were back home in

California that the Mexican government had indeed confiscated *everything* of which the production was in possession, and that Spottiswoode and the rest of our American crew had been locked in a Chiapas jail for a couple days before they were given stiff fines and released.

Medavoy's expertise was enough to ensure that the picture made money—at least once the international box office was tallied—but the critical response was mixed. Roger Ebert wrote that it was "surprisingly, one of the year's best films." But Vincent Canby said the film "means well but it is fatally confused." Personally, although I certainly didn't like every film in which I acted, I was enormously impressed by *Under Fire* when I first saw it, and I couldn't believe that a film that good could have risen out of the ashes of our Mexico shoot.

I seldom find myself siding with producers but I credit Mike Medavoy for ensuring that what might have been a disaster in every way became a film I'll always be proud of. Mike once famously quipped that the Hollywood film industry "is a business that eats its elders instead of its young." He was right about that, and although I had turned forty-two, I was still lucky enough to be perceived as a "young" actor. But the truth was that I was beat up. Legs and I had been living large for several years by now, and the intensity with which we partied had taken a real toll. I'd made a lot of movies in only a few years, and after completing each one I needed at least a month—often much longer—to get back to a state of equilibrium. And once I was home and *Under Fire* was behind me, I was utterly exhausted.

Although Legs and I had settled in Malibu by now, I couldn't stay home and simply recuperate because, she contended, I *had* to go to West Virginia to help one of her family members celebrate his birthday, as I'd done in previous years. She would stay home from the boys' weekend and tend to her own adventures. Our marriage was in a very precarious condition, as she was a young woman committed to a life of hard partying and I was feeling like an old man tiring of the scene rapidly. We were leading separate lives, yet Uncle Bachir, one of Legs's favorite relatives, was someone I liked to support if I could.

Bachir was a storied gambler—the guy could throw craps like nobody's business—yet more than once I had to go and buy his house back for him. He wanted me to return to Charleston, where he and his wife, Jenny, hailed from. As he'd done in previous years, Bachir wanted a bachelor birthday party and let it be known that Nick Nolte was in town—news that would attract high-ranking partygoers to his legendary soiree as well as the girls who would keep them entertained.

At first I refused to go, but when Legs pressed me hard I finally relented. In a telephone call from Malibu, I told Bachir, "I'll go under one condition. You must provide me with a full bottle of pharmaceutical cocaine. I know you guys can get it because there are about five dentists in that group of yours." Bachir wasn't happy, but he and his buddies reluctantly agreed, so I went. Legs stayed home to go partying with her friends the Carbinol brothers, who happened to run a gang in East L.A.

I was already exhausted when I arrived in West Virginia, and the quality and quantity of cocaine that was waiting for me wasn't helping a bit. Seriously strung out, and in real need of help, I began to panic. Bachir had put me up in a friend's palatial house on a golf course, in a red-velvet room with a heart-shaped bathtub, and there were always several goons around whose only job seemed to be making sure that I didn't go anywhere. But when I learned that Bachir and company had even taken out ads in the local paper offering the pleasure of my company at their party, I knew I *had* to escape. I didn't want to involve the police because Bachir was still family and my nose wasn't exactly clean, pun intended. But I knew I had to get out.

One afternoon, a young woman named Terri came in to check whether I needed anything. She looked trustworthy and I took a chance. "You know, I am in a dire situation here," I quietly said to her.

"Yes, you are," she agreed.

I asked if she would help me escape and she said, "No, I don't have the guts to do that. But my sister is coming by. Her name is Rebecca and she has the guts. If she thinks it's right, she will do it."

"Well, how will I know her?" I asked.

"She'll be the prettiest girl you've ever seen," Terri said matter-of-factly.

About three hours later, Rebecca arrived, and she quickly agreed with Terri and me. "You're in a really terrible situation here. The word is out all over town that people ought to come hang out with you. But I'll help. What do I need to do?"

I had a plan. I told Rebecca that I had just a single bag, and that I'd crawl out the bedroom window as soon as she pulled her car around to the side of the house. Then I'd jump in with her and hope she could take me someplace where no one could find me.

And the plan worked. I popped out the window's screen, jumped to the ground, and got into Rebecca's car, and we sped away. She took me to her parents' big house and secreted me in her bedroom. She was twenty-three or so but was living at home, and it didn't take long for her parents to catch on that she was hiding someone in her room.

Words were spoken. In the midst of them, and despite her parents' disapproval, Rebecca confessed that yes, there was a man in her room whom she was helping recover from some trouble. She was doing him a favor, she explained, and that was simply the way it was going to be. She brought me food and checked on me often during the following several days, and when I finally met her parents they were perfectly friendly, and I tried to express my gratitude. "Dr. and Mrs. Linger, I want to thank you," I told them. "Your daughter has quite literally saved me from a very difficult situation, one I had no control over. She helped me get away from this criminal element I was around, and I will leave soon. I'll go home and get everything taken care of."

The doctor and his wife were gracious in turn, telling me that I had been welcome in their home, and the next day I scheduled a flight back to California. But before I departed, I told Rebecca that I was going to get straight and get a divorce. I told her I was terrible about staying in touch by phone, but that I'd call once during the summer—which I did—then added that I hoped she would come stay with me in New York in the fall, where I'd be shooting a film with Katharine Hepburn.

I lived alone in Malibu during that summer; my mother and sister had rented a house on the point, and I climbed into one of the rooms and hid. The divorce proceedings were turned over to the lawyers. Legs's parents were quite upset—their son-in-law Nick had been their meal ticket, after all—but Legs wasn't mad. She received a healthy percentage of my film income from while we were together, and then she was on to the next party she could find—and she always managed to find men everywhere, if she needed any. My mother and sister helped make sure I was okay, and by the time I left for New York that fall, I had ended my second marriage and was sure that better days were on their way.

Chapter 11
Down and Out

Katharine Hepburn had complimented me. Back during the time when we were making *North Dallas Forty*, my agent had called to say, "Nick, she watched *Rich Man, Poor Man* and was very impressed with you. She has a piece of material she wants you to read, and she drove to your house and threw it over your backyard fence. I guess she doesn't go the normal route. She hasn't heard anything from you and she's getting a little feisty."

I looked around the yard and, sure enough, there was the script the legendary actress had "dropped off." It was titled *The Ultimate Solution of Grace Quigley,* and it had been rained on a few times, but I could read it, and I was impressed. The idea of costarring in a film with Katharine Hepburn was fantastic. Lou quickly arranged a meeting at Hal Ashby's Malibu beach house, and when I arrived I was eager to finally meet the renowned director as well as Katharine and the script's writer, Martin Zweiback. Ashby's much-heralded films included *Harold & Maude, Shampoo,* and *Coming Home,* among others, and I presumed he would be directing this new film, too. My good fortune seemed unbelievable.

I quickly learned that Hal would only be producing the film, because, he explained to me, he had done similar stories and didn't want to repeat himself as a director. He wanted Zweiback himself to direct, and Katharine was fine with that choice, but I was young and dumb. I was too green to know that writer-directors can be the best possible people to work for. When you're shooting and the story runs into problems, the director can simply reshape the script as needs demand—it's great.

I didn't know how much I didn't know, so I turned down the film. Five years and a ton of vital experience later, I knew better, and I was surprised that the story still hadn't become a film. I was able to reach Katharine by telephone in New York, and she was quite cordial. "Listen," I told her, "if you don't like me anymore, that's all right, but if you do like me and you want to make that movie, you choose the director and I will accept whomever you choose. You know the type of director this material needs and I don't, so I will accept who you want."

Rather miraculously, Katharine was still very keen to make the movie. She chose Anthony Harvey to direct. He had directed her in *The Lion in Winter* back in 1968 and was a close friend of hers, if not a superb director, yet I knew he could handle this particular material well, so I quickly agreed to do it.

When I met Katharine for the second time at her apartment in New York, she graciously invited me in and asked me to pick the chair in which I wanted to sit. I chose a big, overstuffed armchair, and she lit up. "Ah, yes, just as I thought you would," she exclaimed. "You picked Spence's chair!" She was referring to her long-deceased love, Spencer Tracy. I was utterly charmed. During the time I spent with her that afternoon, she shared her strong belief that a person can't have a successful relationship and be an actor.

"What about between roles and films?" I asked.

"There is no in between," she sharply announced. "There should be a law against you having a relationship, because you love your work, and it's not going to be fair to anybody. You know, Nick, these relationships that we get involved in, people have stereotyped thinking that they are husband and wife and they are going to be together 'til death do you part, and that is not the way life works. Spiritual love is what love is. Relationship love is not love because it breaks down and decays. Acting is such a self-involved thing that there is really no place for a partner." My divorce from Legs wasn't yet final but soon would be, and that day I realized Katharine was not only a superb actor but also someone who was quite wise. She was amazing.

We weren't under way with the new film for long before its title began to be problematic. "Ultimate Solution" was simply too reminiscent of a Nazi phrase for the extermination of Jews, and the much simpler *Grace Quigley* became the better choice, especially because Israeli producers Yoram Globus and Menahem Golan and their company Cannon Films had acquired the rights from Ashby and Zwieback during the long hiatus since I first read the rain-wrinkled script.

The story is a black comedy about an elderly widow who lives alone in a dreary New York City apartment, and who has twice tried and failed to commit suicide. When she sees my character, a Vietnam vet named Seymour Flint, conducting a professional hit one day, she decides to blackmail me into killing her, but not before I off several of her friends who are old, alone, and tired of living, too. It was a suicide-by-hit-man piece, and it could have been dreadful without some-

one of Katharine's stature and talent holding it together. *Grace Quigley* was her final leading role for the
big screen, and more than three decades later, I'm still
hugely grateful for the opportunity to work with her.

She was unique, of course, and always full of surprises. When one of our producers made the mistake
one day of asking her how she planned to play a particular scene, she retorted, "What do you mean how am I
going to play this? Do you know how you're going to do
something before you do it? That's a stupid question!"
She did not suffer fools and always spoke her mind—as
a result she was fired from eight different films, and
once bought her way out of a Broadway play she determined was destined to be a dismal flop.

I received her wrath more than a time or two—like
the morning when I showed up hungover and inex-
cusably late for a scheduled shoot after a long night
of carousing with friendly FBI agents who had been
showing me the underbelly of the city. She was as
angry as she could be and she dressed me down in
her raspy staccato. "You are irresponsible, Nick. You
don't care one bit, do you?"

When I told her I was sorry, she snapped back, "I
don't want to hear da, da, da, Nick. I won't have it!"
Later, when she had calmed down a bit and we had
finished the morning's scene, she approached me more

softly. "Now listen, Nick," she said, "you know Spencer drank, and we had a dickens of a time with Spencer. But he never drank when he was working. You've got to have plenty of sleep. I can get you some Thorazine."

She was kidding, of course—Thorazine would knock me or anyone out for a week! It was for psychotic people who break down so badly they must be strapped down. So when she walked away, I thought, Wow. Okay, tomorrow no more booze. Point taken, Ms. Hepburn.

Katharine Hepburn wasn't the only person who was worried about me at that time. During my marriage to Legs, and for many years before, for that matter, I had been working hard and playing hard, and often combining the two in ways that led to some pretty creative kinds of chaos. My career as an actor had skyrocketed to heights I had never imagined, but instead of finding peace and a degree of meaning in my success, I continued to find life offstage and away from the cameras challenging.

I had grown up among drinkers. Like the rest of their generation, my parents and their friends would party throughout entire weekends, and us kids would watch. Cruising in the car, my mother would put the glove box down and put the box lock on. The ice was there, the booze, the mixing glasses, and she would whip up drinks for her and Dad. It was a 1948 DeSoto, and I'd be in the backseat underneath the blankets, scared to death. That was the way you were supposed to travel. That was not against the law. If an officer stopped you and he saw a family having a few drinks, he wasn't going to say a word. There was no reason to separate the activity of driving and drinking. It wasn't until later when that changed.

Learning the craft of acting and working diligently to perfect it for several decades had given me purpose and focus and a sense of self-worth, but with increasing levels of success had come ever bigger internal trials that I wasn't good at solving. I was still anxious, shy, and highly sensitive. So, I drank—and often drank prodigiously—and self-medicated with drugs in ways that, by the time of the *Grace Quigley* shoot, caused a number of people close to me to presume I was in trouble.

People magazine published a 1984 article in which my friend and fellow actor JoBeth Williams averred, "The man does know how to drink. He's a real good-time guy, but underneath it all there's a danger—that sense that he might explode." My longtime buddy Gary Busey—who often flirted with the abyss himself, of course—saw it a bit differently but essentially agreed with her. "I wouldn't say Nick has a drinking problem. I see it more as a drinking opportunity. It gives him an opportunity—through drinking—to see the best in life."

I drank in those days in order to deal with anything I found difficult—relationships, failed projects—using alcohol as a pain medication, suffering medication, love medication, even as a tonic against loneliness and the ironic kind of isolation that celebrity often brings. I used it for everything and, in my version of my life story at the time, saw it as a friend.

I'm not sure when I first tried cocaine. My generation had embraced psychedelics, and if marijuana seemed to promise the euphoric enjoyment of life, then peyote, mushrooms, and LSD clearly offered enlightenment. I respected plant medicine and the connection it brought to the natural world. But coke was simply an enabler, allowing me to push the limits of my adventures and antics to extreme levels.

I moved in a very fast world in L.A., and I worked in an industry that emphasized things that simply weren't that important—so the coke fit right in. It mimicked a certain kind of creative fire that ultimately burns you out, and, for me, it narrowed my awareness rather than expanding it.

The reason I started taking drugs early in the

sixties was to expand my consciousness. As long as they provided me that feeling, they worked well. But through the years it became a self-centered activity, and I started using harder drugs to close off the pain and suffering of life—in other words, to escape life. Yet for a long time I was able to convince myself that all coke did was make me a better creator, a better actor, as well as intensify my experiences and crank me up in ways I'd enjoyed since the grade school days when my mom would give me a speed "vitamin" to get me to go to school. Much later I learned when the addict finally gives up drugs/goes clean, the whole world opens up emotionally, because he has closed himself down so much.

A few days before the *Grace Quigley* shoot began, I again called Rebecca Linger, the young woman in West Virginia who had hidden me in her bedroom at her parents' house a few months before. I had been thinking about her and found myself missing her calm presence. "You're not here," I told her. "I wish you were here."

Rebecca said she appreciated my calling during the summer, as I had promised, but I hadn't called again, and she couldn't presume that I would, so she had enrolled for a new semester of college, which would begin before long, and in the meantime she was continuing to work in her father's medical office.

"Well, you can always go to school," I advised. "That's no big deal. But I'm up here, and New York is very nice in the fall. Please come up and stay with me. I'd love that."

When they had met me a few months before, Rebecca's parents had encountered a strung-out Hollywood actor who was married and who looked like a wild man—this I understood. And when they learned that I had invited their twenty-three-year-old daughter to join me in a romantic liaison in New York City, they might have gone through the roof, telling their beloved Rebecca that she would be *crazy* to say yes to my offer. They might have forbidden her, futilely, to go—but they trusted her and did neither. Soon Rebecca was with me at the Mayflower Hotel on Central Park West, and I was happy.

Yes, I was still drinking hard at the end of virtually every day's shoot, and yes, there was always plenty of coke around. Dancing on the edge seemed to be a requirement of the creative work I did. Booze and coke helped me stay internally off balance, and the more off balance I was, the more dangerous I could make things for myself, the sharper my concentration as an actor.

And Becky was drawn to that. She believed she could help me—at least a bit—and that perhaps it was her role to try.

Becky got pregnant during the *Grace Quigley* shoot, and when she shared the news with me I was profoundly happy. I had fallen for her and I felt calmer and more secure with her than I had in a very long time. Everything was less chaotic somehow, and I loved the idea of creating a family with her. My divorce was final, and then I had another picture to shoot—this one a kind of *Broadcast News* set in the classroom. I would have the lead role in *Teachers,* which was directed by Arthur Hiller, whose films included *Love Story, The Hospital,* and *Silver Streak.* Rebecca joined me in Malibu and Charleston during the short break I had between movies, then traveled with me to Columbus, Ohio, where we shot *Teachers* in a classic old Midwestern school.

In the midst of the shoot, I was able to finagle a few days off—a real luxury that normally wasn't even thinkable. But Becky was five months pregnant and it was time to make her an honest woman. I rented a Lear jet and we flew to good ol' Lake Tahoe, where a few friends and family members joined us for a simple ceremony. At twenty-three, it was Rebecca's first marriage; it was my third at forty-two, and I believed that starting a family with Rebecca was going to give my life something essential it had always been missing.

Becky's pregnancy was a normal one, and both of us grew increasingly excited as the baby's birth approached in May 1984. But as she went into labor in Charleston, West Virginia, Rebecca expressed concern that the baby wasn't moving every few minutes, as it had for many months before. Doctors examined her and pronounced everthing fine, but she remained really worried.

Rebecca's parents had arrived and her father, a physician, examined her, and he could hear a strong heartbeat and was sure the baby was fine. Her brother, a doctor, too, also was certain there was nothing to worry about, and we did our best to set our minds at ease as Becky's labor intensified.

I will never forget the moment when Rebecca's obstetrician found me in the hospital's expectant-fathers waiting room, walked over, and informed me in a sad but matter-of-fact voice that the baby—a girl—had died sometime before she was delivered. He couldn't pinpoint the cause, he said, and he told me how sorry he was, and there was virtually nothing else that could be said. Needless to say, we were devastated.

When Rebecca was strong enough to leave the hospital a day or so later, we moved her to her parents' house, and her father gave her an injection of Demerol. When her parents left us alone, I gave myself a matching injection of Demerol, and for the following two weeks, the two of us curled up together, never leaving the bed in which we lay.

We were shattered. There is simply no other word to describe it. Rebecca had to physically recover, of course, and both of us had to find the strength to carry on emotionally, as a couple and as individuals. I was numb, then terribly depressed, then angry. I prayed a lot, which was something I never otherwise did, and with the help of a synthesizer keyboard, I even composed a sad song—a Western, cowboy-loses-it-all kind of thing.

By the time we got home to our house in Malibu a few weeks later, I had begun to drink heavily again. Virtually nothing—even my life with Rebecca—seemed to matter, and it was hard to imagine the future. I didn't a give a fuck about anything, and I spent my days chain-smoking, drinking, questioning my existence, and wishing I could find a way to make the searing pain go away. Rebecca did what she could to remind me that we remained the best things that had ever happened to each other, and, of course, she was right. But I was still diving into dark, dark waters.

———————

A few months later, a project came my way that I couldn't turn down. Touchstone, the new company at Disney that had been formed to make pictures for adults, was beginning its run with a satire based on the 1932 French comedy *Boudu sauvé des eaux.* The new film, written and directed by the renowned filmmaker Paul Mazursky, was to be titled *Down and Out in Beverly Hills,* and the part Paul offered me was the guy who was down and out. Jack Nicholson had said no to the role, and I wanted to do it. I *had* to begin working again at some point; we would be shooting at home in Southern California, my costars would be my old friend Richard Dreyfuss and the singular Bette Midler, and the opportunity to work with a writer-director like Paul seemed to be an enormous one.

The smart money at the time was on the likelihood that Touchstone would fail. Wall Street was convinced that the Disney brand had been exclusively linked to children for too long, and that a Disney adult division would never work—regardless of the quality of the films it produced. But Michael Eisner had left Paramount to head Disney, in part, to prove the smart money wrong. And he had done something brilliant, it seemed to me, by selecting Paul to direct Touchstone's first picture.

Paul had grown up in Beverly Hills, and it made perfect sense to adapt the original French story of a rich but dysfunctional couple who save the life of a suicidal homeless man, and set it in a place he both loved and hated, and that he knew so well. It was one of Paul's best satires, and he was a satirist, no question about it. He had a lot to say about society.

The story begins with my character Jerry Baskin wandering into the backyard of the palatial home of Dave and Barbara Whiteman, jumping into their pool to commit suicide. But Dave, played by Dreyfuss, saves Jerry and becomes intrigued by his past and how he spiraled so "down and out." Paul encouraged me to draw from my own background as I created the Jerry character, and that was a big help. It was damn funny irony that Jerry's most recent setback is that he has failed at becoming an actor! I dug in, injecting elements of my own life story into my character—which I did as often as my directors would let me get away with it, and in this case Paul told me to go for it. One such moment came as my character eats a real meal for the first time in months and he explains to Dave that his troubles began long before, back when he was busted for selling fake draft cards and was convicted of a felony. Sound familiar?

In order to really get into the role, I was sleeping

outside in a homeless section of Los Angeles for two nights before getting a bed in a mission shelter. But it didn't take me more than about seven hours out on the streets to turn into a space cadet—it was intense—and when I tried the shelter, I discovered that I couldn't have a bed. I didn't have the seniority.

I didn't bathe for a couple of weeks. I never want to wash a character off, so to speak, at the end of a day's shoot. There's an important feeling I get from a certain amount of dirt. And it's very difficult for me to take a shower and scrub myself clean one day, then come back the next and put on fake dirt and pretend that I've been sleeping outside. You're not physically in touch with it, not emotionally in touch with it. You don't know what it's like to wake up with the sun on your face.

But Bette was disgusted by me. "He's filthy! I can't work with him," she complained to Paul, who then winked at me. "Keep it up!" he said. "She's already into her part and we haven't shot anything yet." Needless to say, Bette and more than a few others on the set were also horrified when they saw me eating real dog food—something my character Jerry is forced to do to survive. I had to search around a good bit to find canned dog food I liked better than the Dinty Moore beef stew I was provided, but I finally found some.

And wouldn't you know it? Mike, the border collie who played the Whitemans' beloved pet Matisse in the film, was a vegetarian and had never eaten meat in his life. His trainer was quite upset that I had meat in my portion in a scene in which the dog and I eat from side-by-side bowls, but it turned out not to be a problem because Mike wouldn't go near my meaty stuff. He only wanted to eat from *his* bowl—and I ate from mine. No kidding.

It was something of a stroke of genius for Paul to cast Little Richard as the Whitemans' eccentric next-door neighbor Orvis Goodnight. The role is a cameo but the legendary singer shines, although he struggled with a long speech in which he rants at the Beverly Hills police about not protecting him in the same way they do his white neighbors. He worked through take after take on a Friday afternoon to deliver his speech with righteous anger and without a single flub, but a word or two always kept tripping him up.

Finally, he called Paul over to his limousine and said, "You know, Paul, I'm Jewish," and Paul acknowledged that yes, he was aware of that.

"Well, the Sabbath's about to begin and I can't work on the Sabbath."

But we *had* to get the scene shot, so Paul implored

him. "You know, Little Richard, I'm Jewish, too, and if we both get on our knees and pray, I'm sure we'll be forgiven for a tiny little bit of work on the Sabbath." So, they prayed, and Little Richard nailed his speech and Paul got the shot.

Paul was always on the lookout for something unusual, something out of the ordinary. And he wouldn't let any of us get away with our usual shtick. When Richard Dreyfuss—whom I had called Lumpy for years—would throw in one of the little twists that were his stock in trade, Paul would say, "No, no, Richard, let's leave that out." And he was very gentle with Bette. She had been nominated for an Academy Award for *The Rose* but had been treated like dirt on her next picture, *Jinxed!* She was feeling fragile and Paul made sure all of us were particularly kind to her so she could get her confidence back—and we were, and she did. Some filmmakers can be real pigs. Especially with actresses. But not Paul.

The fun part for me was transforming my character from a guy who's so desperate he wants to call it a day into a man who, with Dave Whiteman's help, comes to understand both himself and his hosts so well that he's able to wrap them around his fingers. I loved the satire on power and prestige and the development of equality after those roles have been reversed. Jerry and Dave help each other out of their own sadnesses and are renewed with hope and vigor for life. It was a perfect role for me at that moment in time because at last I was ready to *live* again. I was blessed and my bowl of dog food was overflowing.

Chapter 12
Family

*D*own and *Out in Beverly Hills* was an enormous success. Critics said it was one of the freshest satires produced in years. The picture, which had cost about $14 million to make, earned more than $62 million in the U.S. alone. And it had been damn good for me personally, bringing humor back into my life as well as introducing me to the brilliance of Paul Mazursky, who would remain my dear friend until his death twenty-eight years later. The role had helped my career as well. I was in demand and able to stay out of trouble working only on projects I believed in.

Rebecca continued to bring nurturing stability to my life. Our age difference didn't get in our way and she was a good and calming influence on me. She became pregnant again and six months after *Down and Out* was released, our beautiful and perfectly healthy son,

Brawley, was born. Our shared relief and excitement helped heal the deep hurt of past losses. For the first time in my life I experienced unconditional love in the way that only a parent can. It was wonderful.

For the next five years, the three of us were a *family* and I always took them with me whenever I needed to shoot away from Los Angeles. I made eight pictures during that time—some more memorable than others—yet I continued to accept only roles in which I saw a story worth telling, a character that I wanted to explore, a challenge I hadn't encountered, or an opportunity for me to stretch and to grow.

Scorsese was great to work with. Marty directed me as abstract painter Lionel Dobie in *New York Stories,* three one-acts bundled into a film about life in the Big Apple. Scorsese, Francis Ford Coppola, and Woody Allen each told a separate story in the film. My segment was a great little study of an artist, especially a painter. I hung with a few during that time and they would say that painting is a physical activity; you must attack the canvas and engage it intimately and physically. It was as if they spoke of acting.

Unfortunately, having three stories bundled together was so unusual for American audiences that they focused on comparing the three instead of seeing them for their own individual merits and the film did not fare well. Regardless, it was a treat for me to work with Marty.

As the self-indulgent painter in *New York Stories*, my hair was long and I was bearded and heavy—a bit of a paunchy bear. A couple of years later, I was buff and clean-shaven and I wanted to work with Scorsese again, this time on his planned remake of *Cape Fear*, the 1962 film starring Robert Mitchum and Gregory Peck. Scorsese already had cast his friend and longtime colleague Robert De Niro as the revenge-obsessed rapist and ex-convict Max Cady. I wanted the role of the lawyer who Cady believes is responsible for his imprisonment, and whom Cady wants to destroy.

I don't think Marty could see me in the role of lawyer Sam Bowden. I'm thinking when my name would come up for it Marty would say he didn't want a big beefy bear (like in *New York Stories*); it had to be a sharp lawyer type. So I decided to show him I *was* the role. I always seem to stick my head in at just the right moment. That was especially true on *Cape Fear*. To help make my case to Marty, I told my assistant Billy Cross we were going to the premiere party for Marty's new film *Goodfellas*, starring De Niro, Ray Liotta, and Joe Pesci. I told Billy, "Let's get our best suits on and go!"

The room was packed with people, and Billy and I stood against a wall quietly watching, doing our best to look like unassuming lawyers in expensive suits. Marty walked past us a couple of times without noticing me—which I took to be a good sign—before he walked past us a third time, stopped in his tracks, turned to me, and exclaimed, "Nick!"

I introduced him to Billy and congratulated him on his new film, and Marty quickly wanted to bring Bob De Niro over to say hello. One of the shyest people I've ever known, Bob simply shook my hand and in a soft voice said it was nice to meet me before he walked away. But I could see Marty's mind churning. He wanted to know if I could stop by his office the following day, and I said absolutely I could.

I added a pair of eyeglass frames (with no glass in them) to my professional look before I met Marty at noon the following day. Bob was in his office as well, and the three of us talked for a bit about *Cape Fear* and its challenges and opportunities. I told them I was sure it was going to be a great piece; Marty asked if I would be interested in the lawyer role, and I told him by God, I was *very* interested. So, he cast me, and I couldn't wait to play a part that Marty and others initially didn't think was right for me—big bear or not.

Nicholas King Nolte, 1941. "U.S. enters WWII."

Photo courtesy of the author

My father, Franklin Arthur "Lank" Nolte.

Photo courtesy of the author

TOP: My mother, Helen King Nolte, modeling for Chicago department store. Could have been Capone's wife.

BOTTOM: Helen King Nolte and her dog. "Get on with the picture so I can go into the woods and play."

Photos courtesy of the author

TOP: Me on the far left. My imagination full of Davy Crockett and wild adventures.
Private collection of Neal Tarman, courtesy of Ames Historical Society

BOTTOM: My sister and me in Ames, Iowa.
Photo courtesy of the author

TOP: Kicking for Westside High, Omaha, Nebraska, 1959.
BOTTOM: Kathy Carney, my first love.

My first mug shot. Draft card debacle.

Self-timed photo for my theater portfolio, Phoenix.

Photo courtesy of the author

Self-shot for Actors Inner Circle portfolio photo, 1968.
Photo courtesy of the author

Allen Dutton includes me in his landscapes during the LSD year.
Photo by Allen Dutton

Allen Dutton—in front of instead of behind the camera for once—and I play two peasants who screw up everything in a Christmas play for Phoenix Theater.

The cast of a Tennessee Williams's play. Actors Inner Circle. My first wife, Sheila Page, on the far right.

Photo courtesy of the author

ABOVE: Backstage preparing for *Winterset*. Little Theatre of the Rockies.

BELOW: On the set of *The Deep* with Jackie Bisset.
The Deep: © 1978 *Ulvis Alberts/mptvimages.com*

TOP: Karel Reisz and I discuss *Who'll Stop the Rain,* 1977.
© *Bruce McBroom/mptvimages.com*

BOTTOM: Hitting the town with my second wife, Legs.
Ron Galella/WireImage

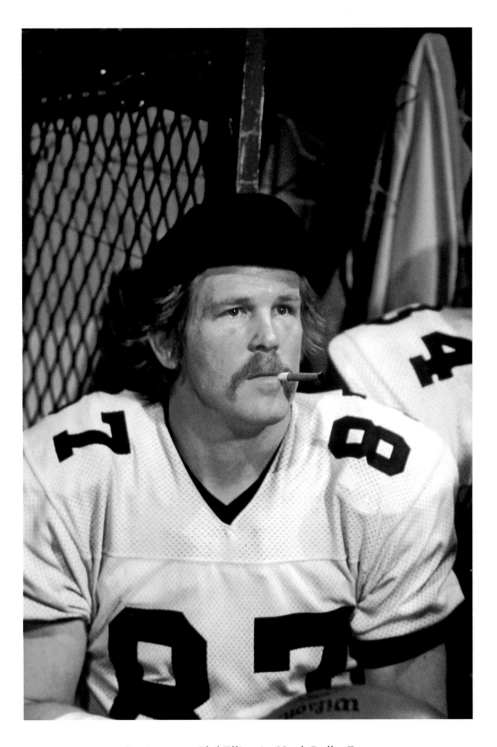

Gearing up as Phil Elliott in *North Dallas Forty*.
North Dallas Forty: © *1978 Mel Traxel/mptvimages.com*

TOP: The legendary Katharine Hepburn and I on *Grace Quigley*.
Photo by John Seakwood

BOTTOM: Eddie Murphy, director Walter Hill, and me on *Another 48 Hrs*.
Photo by Bruce W. Talamon/Paramount Studios/Hollywood Historic Photos

TOP: My Wife Rebecca, myself, and Barbra Streisand after a private screening of *Prince of Tides* for Princess Diana.

Photo by Tim Graham/Getty Images

BOTTOM: Marty Scorsese and I are spellbound by Robert Mitchum's coolness on set of *Cape Fear*.

Photo by Phillip Caruso/mptvimages.com

One of my favorite authors, Kurt Vonnegut, with director Keith Gordon and me on the set of *Mother Night*, 1995.

Licensed by: Warner Bros. Entertainment Inc. All Rights Reserved.

Vicki Lewis and I attend 1999 Film Critics Awards for *Affliction*.

Photo by UPI/Newscom

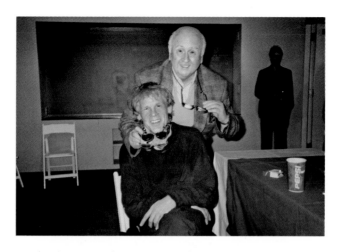

TOP: Bryan O'Byrne and I are reunited at the 2000 Sundance Festival.
Photo courtesy of the author

BOTTOM: Partner Clytie Lane and I attend "An Evening for Africa" in 2010.
Photo by Florian Seefried/Getty Images

TOP: My son Brawley accompanies me to the Academy Awards for the *Warrior* nomination.

Photo by George Pimentel/WireImage

BOTTOM: My daughter Sophie and me on the set of *Luck*.

Photo courtesy of the author

Rebecca and I had purchased a hilltop house outside Charleston, West Virginia, so she could see her family often, and we spent a lot of time there. And when Marty told me I'd need to research small-town lawyers because he knew nothing about them or the day-to-day work they did, I was way ahead of him. I had already driven around much of the state, visiting small courts, getting to know the clerks, and they would tell me when an interesting case was about to go to trial, and I'd be sure to be on hand to watch the lawyers at work in the courtroom, and watch how the judges presided, too.

One time I got a call from a clerk I'd created a good rapport with, and she had news she eagerly wanted to share. "I've got a real good one for you, Nick," she told me. "This girl was on a paper route on her bike and her boyfriend pulled up in his car, knocked her off the bike, and raped her. Then he bit her cheek and took a hunk of flesh, spit it at her, and shouted, 'I got you now, bitch!' Rape isn't really about sex."

"Jesus, I'm getting that," I responded, and, of course, I immediately wanted to discuss the case with Marty and Bob. They both responded in the way I was sure they would. Bobby was stunned for a while before he turned to Marty and said, "We've got to add this. We've got to do this," and so they did, revising the storyline of the character played by Illeana Douglas to include Max Cady giving her a grisly bite during their sex scene.

Jessica Lange, who played my wife in the film, was great to work with. She and I really clicked on-screen right from the start of our shoot, and off-screen we had a ball. Sometimes we fell into crazy laughter as we would slip and fall on our asses in all the blood Marty insisted on soaking the set with—it was a bloody picture, after all. Our daughter was beautifully played by Juliette Lewis. When we broke for Christmas, she flew home to Los Angeles, where her boyfriend Brad Pitt promptly broke up with her. She was heartbroken and angry, and when shooting started again early in January, she did what you might expect a teenage girl to do: she took all her emotions out on her dad—at least her make-believe dad, and that was me. She repeatedly wanted me to know that I wasn't half the actor Bob De Niro was, and she found a way to give me shit on the set virtually every day. It was just like parenthood!

Despite his shyness and need to be alone a lot of the time, I got to know Bob well, and I liked him. He isn't someone who could, or would even want to, make small talk. He isn't dazzled by celebrity—his own or others'—and I think what connected us both was the way in which each of us "hides" inside the characters we play. We may not be the sorts of guys who would hang out with each other on the street. However, we do share an immense satisfaction in playing characters that liberate us from our own shyness.

No one works harder at the craft of acting than Bob. I found out the kind of complexity that he goes through to be extremely prepared. His focus, his hours, his obsession with the role he is creating is legendary, and I observed it on the set of *Cape Fear*. To portray Max Cady to the depths he demanded, Bob would get out of bed at midnight and work out with weights for ninety minutes or so, then go back to bed before getting up at four to begin two full hours of makeup. By the end of the shoot, the stress he was under brought Bob near a breaking point, yet he channeled everything he was experiencing into Max's terrifying expression of evil—a role that led to both Golden Globe and Oscar nominations for best actor on a film that made all of us who were part of it proud.

We shot much of *Cape Fear* in Fort Lauderdale, Florida, and during the shoot Rebecca became intrigued with buying a house there; then she really began to pressure me. But the idea just didn't make sense. "Rebecca, we have a house in North Carolina," I told her. "We have a house in West Virginia, and we have our house in California. We never get to some of these houses, and I really don't have any interest in coming back to Fort Lauderdale."

What I didn't know—really couldn't know without her explaining it to me—was that for a West Virginia girl like her, having a house on the Atlantic coast in South Florida was the ultimate, an accomplishment that would outshine any other. So, she persisted.

I agreed to let her show me a couple of houses, yet I was focused entirely on *Cape Fear*. I was working fifteen hours a day every day, and I would come home to our rental house and simply collapse. I was working so hard, we barely saw one another. One day, when I didn't have to be on the set, I looked for Rebecca but I couldn't find her. Brawley was in West Virginia visiting his grandparents, but I couldn't track down his mom anywhere.

I asked my assistant—my sister Nancy's son, Eric—if he knew where she was, and he didn't. Then I had an idea, a feeling that I had to investigate. I took Eric with me and we drove to the house that Rebecca had liked best. A SOLD banner had been added to the FOR SALE sign, and a car was parked out front. "Oh, Jesus," I said to my nephew, "she's bought this house."

We got out of our car and walked toward the front door. Although the living room drapes were drawn, I could see through a crack in them, and what I saw inside was Rebecca sitting on a sofa kissing some guy. "Oh, shit, this sucks," I whispered to Eric in a rush of emotion. Then, I went to the front door and knocked, and Rebecca gasped when she opened the door and saw me standing there.

"Uh, you're not supposed to be here," she said.

"And you're not supposed to be doing what you're doing," I responded. I kept my cool and added, "Look, I'm going back to our house. I'd finish up what you're doing in there, if I were you, and come home. We've got to talk."

"Yeah. Okay. All right," Rebecca said. "I'll see you there."

When I saw her a few minutes later, she knew what she wanted to say. "Look, Nick, I want that house and I want a divorce. I just can't do this anymore."

"Oh, come on, Rebecca," I pleaded. "You don't really want to do this. I mean, we have a son. He's not even six yet. We've got a ways to go before he's out of the house. You don't want to break us all up now. I know you're younger than me, but you're not missing anything out there, believe me. I've got a little knowledge on you here, so please, think about it."

Those kinds of conversations went on for a couple of weeks, but Rebecca did not change her mind. I think she wanted to experience her own freedom, and she was still young at thirty-two. I finally quit trying to convince her to continue our marriage and started spending lots of time in my trailer on set, yelling and kicking things around. I put a sign outside on a garbage can that read, CAMPER DIVORCE, PLEASE DONATE, but the only things the cast and crew contributed were a Canadian quarter and some rocks. Scorsese's parents always had liked to put their trailer next to mine because I was a nice guy and all that. Well, they moved right away when I started taking it all out on the garbage can.

By the time we wrapped *Cape Fear*—a film that would ultimately gross $182 million worldwide—Rebecca and I had set divorce proceedings in motion. We negotiated our dissolution back home in California; I suggested we use a psychiatrist instead of a lawyer—or dozens of lawyers—and Rebecca agreed. I was intent on splitting our lives as easily as possible, and I wrote down everything we owned in chalk on a blackboard and told Rebecca she could pick the half she wanted.

At the end of our time with the psychiatrist, Rebecca announced a final demand, saying, "I've got to take Brawley to Florida with me," and her words hit me hard. As far as I was concerned, the only really great thing about marriage was the children it produced. The love that's engendered in you by your child is what love truly is, I had discovered. I'm not sure I would have died for Rebecca, or any wife, but I readily would have died for Brawley in 1991—and I still would.

I couldn't bear the prospect of being separated from him, but I had to consider his welfare, too, and I knew it would be terrible for us to fight over him. So I agreed that he would live with his mom in Florida but would spend as much time as possible with me, whether at home in Malibu or in whatever location moviemaking had taken me to temporarily. The arrangement was working quite well for a few months until the day I got a telephone call from Rebecca that set us dramatically at odds again.

"Brawley's first-grade teacher has decided that he has ADD and we are going to put him on Ritalin," she declared.

"Oh, no you are not," I responded. "They are *not* going to put him on any amphetamines or Ritalin or anything until I get there. When I get there, I will discuss it with a psychiatrist, with the principal, with the teachers, with you, and then we will make an informed decision. But I am not going to give him something that nobody knows how it works. We are *not* going to do that."

Then I immediately called my mother in Phoenix, asking if she happened to have any Ritalin. When she told me she did, I asked her to get it to me quickly. We were about to complete the filming of *Lorenzo's Oil*—a movie about two parents' effort to find a treatment for their son's very rare neurological disease—in Pittsburgh, and I flew to Fort Lauderdale as soon as I could.

At a meeting with Brawley's teachers and principal and Rebecca and me, they described behaviors that convinced them that he suffered from attention deficit disorder, things like disobeying authority because he claimed he had superpowers. I was unconvinced. I asked if any of them had considered that this little boy has just been through the most traumatic experience he'd had. I said, "His parents have just divorced and he is not comfortable and he is forced to be with you people who he doesn't know. Have you thought that that could be driving this behavior?" They responded that they were professionals, and we were dealing with ADD; they were certain.

So, I asked if any of them had any personal experience with Ritalin and its effects, and when all of them said no, they had never taken the drug, I took out a small bottle and poured some pills on the desk. "Well, then let's each take a ten-milligram capsule and we'll see what it does, and then each of us will be more knowledgeable about how it can or can't help Brawley," I suggested.

This was not an idea to which anyone responded positively, however. "No, no, no, I don't need those pills. I can't take those pills. That doesn't do anything for me," I heard. Each of them knew plenty about Ritalin and its effects without having actually taken the drug.

"So, you're recommending this drug for a child, but you still don't know what it is. How do you figure that works? You are just going to take a shot and maybe mess up his life, is that your intention?" I asked.

I was assured by everyone present that they were intent on *helping* Brawley, not hurting him, but I wouldn't back down. "Here is how we can help him," I said. "You give me a couple of weeks to spend some time with my boy and figure out what is going on and what he's really mad about. I have a pretty good idea. Give me a couple of weeks, and if I can't find a solution to this, then we'll discuss Ritalin at that point. Understood? Because I am not going to agree to anything you have presented. I will not allow it, and I will hold you personally responsible for introducing any drugs into his system." And I just left it at that—a veiled threat that hung in the air as our meeting adjourned.

When *Lorenzo's Oil* was finished I immediately flew to Florida and bought a house down the street from Rebecca's. I started to hang with Brawley. At first, when we began to spend our days together, he wouldn't talk about anything. I purchased a big-ass ragtop convertible Cadillac and the two of us drove around Florida together. When he realized one day that we were approaching his psychiatrist's office, he freaked out, shouting at me that he wouldn't go in. "No. No. No!" he yelled.

"Come on, Brawley," I said, "it's no big deal. We'll just go in and if he doesn't have an answer for us, we won't stay. It's no big deal." I succeeded in getting him inside and Brawley stonewalled, refusing to say a word until I took him down on the carpeted floor of the psychiatrist's office and began to tickle him mercilessly. He tried to escape, and when he couldn't he started to hit me and cry and finally let loose a flurry of words. "I don't want to be here, Dad. I don't like this place, I don't like my mom, I don't like this guy, I don't have any friends here. I wish I had superpowers."

I kept teasing and tickling him. "If you would eat your Wheaties, *then* you might have superpowers," I said, and it made him laugh, and all his frustrations flooded out of him with his laughter. The psychiatrist had been paying very close but silent attention, yet now he interrupted. "We've been working together for almost a year and this is the most he has ever said. But now that he has expressed himself, I see that Brawley is not ADD," he said, reassuring us, and said he would call Rebecca and Brawley's school that afternoon to say that he was just fine.

For the following six years, Brawley continued to live in Florida with his mother, staying with me in Malibu or on set whenever he could. But on the day of his twelfth birthday, he called a limousine service and arranged for a pickup. Then he called the airport and purchased a one-way plane ticket with allowance money I had sent him every year, and held an impromptu birthday party for himself with a few friends. As his friends were leaving the house, Brawley explained to his mother that he would be leaving for the airport in half an hour. He was flying to California, where he would live with me, and he would come stay with her, he explained, on holidays and during the summer.

When Rebecca told him he couldn't do that, Brawley was ready. He knew the law, he told her, and now that he was twelve it allowed him to decide with which parent he wanted to live. It was time to experience life with his dad, and he was ready, he told her, and the limo arrived and a few hours later I met Brawley at LAX, and from then on, he began a new life on his own terms. He had his power back and he was fine. He was strong.

Chapter 13
Turning of the *Tide*

I take storytelling seriously. I've turned down many roles during my career and I've sometimes been called an asshole for doing so. Yet I've always followed a couple of my own rules. The role I'm being offered must be significant somehow; it must have substance to it and pose a challenge for me. And secondly, the story must be worth telling. If you're going to be an actor, then you must be into literature, historical events, and life stories.

When the line producer on the Sidney Lumet film *Q&A* asked me on set one day in 1989 whether I'd read Pat Conroy's bestselling novel *The Prince of Tides*, I confessed that I hadn't. He pressed a copy of the book into my hands and told me I was in for a wonderful experience. I started poring over it, and Jesus, he was right! It was a hell of a book. I could feel something was up, but I didn't know what. Right from the beginning of my read, I felt powerfully linked to the character Tom Wingo, who narrates his family's story.

I imagined that someone would certainly make a movie from it, but which of the book's many characters would a film focus on? How many of the book's extraordinary stories could one film tell? I asked if anyone had drafted a screenplay yet, and the producer said yes, he would get me the script. The script was very good, very focused, and it centered on Tom and the women in his life.

When I next spoke with my agent Sue Mengers I asked if I could meet whoever was planning to direct the film.

"Yes," Sue told me by telephone, "you can. It's Barbra Streisand." Sue may have thought the possibility of working with a female director of Barbra's notoriety would give me pause, but it didn't.

"Okay. Is she going to play a role in it, too?" I asked.

"Yes, she's going to play the psychiatrist Lowenstein, but she's directing, too."

I said, "I've seen her films. They're good."

"And she's seen you," Sue said, "and she'd like you to come over to her house tomorrow night, have a cocktail, and introduce yourself." Once more, it seemed good fortune had come my way. I was in New York, still filming *Q&A,* and I was eager to hear more about Barbra's vision for the book.

When I knocked on her door the next evening, she answered it, and she seemed a bit surprised to see me with jet-black hair and a moustache so big and thick that it hid my mouth. I did *not* look like her image of Tom Wingo, nor my own for that matter, and I quickly explained that I was playing the role of a New York cop in a Sidney Lumet picture at the moment. She invited me in and asked if I would like some wine.

"Yes, I'd love some red wine, if you have it," I said, and she poured me a glass before she showed me around her apartment, which occupied an entire floor of a park-side building in Manhattan. White carpet lay everywhere, and I could tell Barbra was nervous about the possibility that I would spill my wine—so concerned, in fact, that she seemed unable to think about anything else. I made small talk as best I could, getting a kick out of the way in which I was worrying her with the wine in my hand.

Finally, I told her that I loved the material for the new film but I'd better get going—I had an early call in the morning. I tipped back the wineglass and chugged it—not spilling a drop—and I could see the instant relief on her face. Her carpets were safe.

Robert Redford had owned the film rights to *The Prince of Tides* for a while, but he'd had a very different vision for the film's storyline than Barbra. The script that she had created with the help of the novel's author, Pat Conroy, and screenwriter Becky Johnston really found the heart of the material by letting Tom tell the story of the women in his life. It was going to be an epic role for me and I knew I had to prepare for it as immersively as I could.

I moved into a house above Myrtle Beach, South Carolina, not too far from Conroy's hometown of Beaufort, and began to dive into that watery Southern world of kudzu, shrimp, sand, and tradition. I tried to trace Pat Conroy's writing of the novel, which became sort of a massive detective job. Conroy talks about not only Beaufort, but all of the South. Beaufort is a little bit of an exclusive Southern town, so I asked Conroy himself to help me understand a place that seems to always withhold its secrets. With his help, I got permission to teach some classes at Beaufort's high school—because Tom is an English teacher and football coach—and because Tom's father is a shrimper, I spent a month or more hauling nets on the shrimping boats. I got so tan that Barbra worried that my face would be difficult to light next to hers when we started shooting. I attended a couple of parties in Beaufort at Pat's suggestion, too, and I was surprised to encounter some people who were hostile to our project, worried that we would turn their world into a cartoon, and convinced that Barbra was arrogant and that I was a kind of cowboy they wanted nothing to do with.

Before we began shooting, Barbra came to me with a proposition. The studio had balked at spending an un-anticipated million dollars on an added scene, one she thought would contribute a lot to the film. But Barbra never backed down if she could help it, and she ex-plained that we could have our way if each of us kicked in $500,000 so we could shoot it. I agreed to contribute the money—reducing my fee for starring in the film dramatically—because I knew that if I had said no she would have viewed my response as a lack of commit-ment to the project. I'm not sure the scene ultimately even got in the film, but my show of support did.

From that moment until the film wrapped, I was immensely impressed with her artistic vision, her passion, and a kind of genius she brought to virtually every aspect of the enormously complex business of making a movie. Barbra had something of a reputa-tion at the time for being mean, but it wasn't that at all. She demanded a lot of everyone with whom she was collaborating. She was totally thorough and prepared, and she did a lot of research. She knew exactly how she wanted to tell the story and was tremendously connected to the material. I liked her discipline. She was never satisfied, and she would always search for more.

My character Tom Wingo's world is shaped by women, and in real life I've tried to understand the strengths and vulnerabilities and needs and beliefs of the women with whom I've been close, albeit not always successfully. Even though I haven't created a fifty-year relationship with one woman, I've been satisfied with my relationships. Some have been fated from the beginning—much like the Lowenstein-Wingo relationship in the film—with a constant underlying tension between romantic love and something that is more human, more enduring. One reason I resonated so strongly with the character of Tom is that he projects Lowenstein as a lover, confidante, mother, nurturer, confessor—everything.

Barbra and I talked extensively about our characters' relationship and about romantic love versus the pull that Tom feels to return home to his family. I had had those conversations about characters' motivations at times with male directors over the years, but this was the first time I was working with a female director. With men, I've always created a kind of collusive agreement about the emotional points of particular scenes and character arcs, but with Barbra, the two of us had to continually explore, and we both welcomed that.

Barbra's incredible determination and willingness to get down in the trenches and fight for what she believed was necessary came from her feminine response to a heavily male-dominated artistic environment. The passion she brought to that battle was part of her brilliance. People on the set would complain, "Oh my God, she's got four versions of this scene!" when she insisted on multiples—planning to select the one that would make the cut only in the editing suite. And it *was* an agonizing process, and I sometimes grew frustrated, but ultimately, she always knew the right way to go.

During our shoot, Barbra told a journalist that I had been her pick to play Tom from the beginning, saying, "Nick approaches a role with raw ferocity, with no concern for how he can get the audience to like him, and that's very admirable. Underneath, he's very complex—full of pain, anger, sweetness, and enormous vulnerability." I was powerfully drawn to her just as she was to me, so much so that I knew that early on we needed to talk about the reasons why we shouldn't slip into a romantic and sexual relationship with each other as we worked.

"You know, Barbra," I told her, "if we get into a

situation where we want to cross the line physically, we shouldn't do it, because it's too dangerous for the film to have to carry a relationship and the story at the same time. We can live in the fantasy of a relationship, and that will survive. But an actual physical relationship might not survive the film. That's been my experience."

She kind of dismissed me at first, saying, "Oh, well. Yes, you're probably right. Let's think about that."

"The reason to talk about it now," I continued, "is because there are going to be moments when it's incredibly tempting, and we have gotten very close." I gave her books by Robert A. Johnson, the Jungian psychiatrist, because he talks about how Chrétien de Troyes describes romantic love as killed when Lancelot seduces King Authur's queen, Guinevere. The minute you have physical contact with the object of your love, you've lost the beauty of your faith. I was trying to be pragmatic. You can love the queen, but you can't touch the queen. And you can worship the queen and fight for the queen. But if you have sex with the queen, you're not half as good a fighter as you would be living on faith.

As the filming of the two characters' growing relationship got under way in earnest, I couldn't help but notice that she would always want me to be naked while she was covered under about ten layers of sweaters. So,

I asked, "How come I've got to show my ass and you never show anything?"

"They don't pay me enough for me to show these tits," she teased.

"They must be some tits," I responded, and we had a good laugh.

During the long months that Barbra edited the film in Los Angeles with Don Zimmerman, she telephoned me at home one day and said, "Come out and live with me."

"Barbra, I can't," I told her. "You know I have a son and—"

"I want to be with you," she interrupted. And suddenly I knew what had happened. She had been watching dailies and working toward creating a final cut day after day for many weeks, and in the process, she had fallen in love with Tom Wingo.

"Barbra, I can't do that. I can't do that," I softly told her.

"Well, what do you want to be to me?" she asked.

And I said, "A good friend."

"You don't know what I ask from my friends," she retorted.

The Prince of Tides was one of the peak experiences of my life as an actor. Critics and audiences were deeply moved by the film when it was released on Christmas Day 1991. A couple of months later, Barbra was nominated for a Golden Globe for best director and I was nominated for best actor. We received seven Academy Award nominations, but unfortunately, Barbra was omitted by her fellow directors because of something political that had happened earlier on an entirely different film.

Barbra was wounded by the snub, and although the Golden Globe nomination meant something to her, ultimately not winning in that category made her pain sharper. I won a Golden Globe for my role as Tom Wingo, and she and I and others in the cast and crew won a number of other awards that winter.

It feels wonderful to be recognized for the quality of your work on the stage or screen—it's tremendous, of course. But I didn't like—and still don't—the concept, the competition of picking which actors have made the best performance of a given year. You just can't make that kind of judgment. It's a popular spectacle and it's highly commercialized—and it smacks of unfairness. I have nothing against a group of actors getting together to honor each other's good work for the year, but I'm opposed to allowing the whole world in on the process. That year I was also named *People* magazine's "Sexiest

Man Alive," which now seems like karmic payback for my grumpy view of awards.

Barbra was a force of nature to work for, and she made a damn fine film that will be watched and appreciated for many years to come. And like Lowenstein, she helped facilitate a period of my life where there was a balance between what I gained from the stories I inhabited over the years and how much I was willing to contribute of myself.

Chapter 14
Against Type

When Brawley came to live with me in Malibu when he was twelve, I gave him two options as we began this new phase of our lives together. "Do you want an open house or a closed house?" I asked. "In an open house, we allow people to come in, but we have rules. There's a bedtime rule during the school week and we allow a certain limited number in the open house. But in an open house, you can have some friends living with you. In a closed house, there's none of that. You go to school. You can have friends over for playtime, but they go home by six."

I think he was knocked sideways by my willingness to let him make such a decision, and I wasn't surprised a bit when he said he wanted ours to be an open house. It made sense to me as well, having grown up in an open house myself. Soon after, I became a kind of de facto godparent to two kids who were friends of Brawley's and whose parents needed to move away from Southern California, at least for a time. I hired a tutor for the group—and she was excellent—and other friends who didn't live with us would come over to get the tutor's help with their studies as well. I took great joy in partaking when I was able, teaching them about biology through looking at our own live blood under a dark-field microscope and other hands-on adventures in science.

In 1999, I took Brawley with me to England, where we shot the Merchant Ivory film *The Golden Bowl.* I assured his mother that he would only be gone three months, and that he would study while he was away, and that when we returned we would all reassess the big picture of his education. In London, I had the good fortune to encounter a brilliant tutor named Matt Tromans, whom Brawley loved to be with. I wouldn't see them for days sometimes, and on occasion they wouldn't get home from an excursion 'til the middle of the night. On the days when Brawley would hang out on the set, the art director and wardrobe folks would fight over which department in the film they were going to make him part of—it was great, and you can imagine how pleased and proud I was that my son was doing so well.

As we left a pub one evening to walk back to our hotel, he said, "You know, Dad, I'm not sure if I've really learned much while I've been here."

"Well, Brawley," I told him, "this hasn't been that two-plus-two-equals-four kind of learning. This isn't that kind of education; it's the kind that seeps into you. It's about knowing where you are from. Seeing yourself in the world. You get a different view of America, where you come from, when you're away."

"Yes," he said, understanding something of what I meant, "America is prudish in places, isn't it?"

When we got back to California, we discussed his situation with officials at his school and everyone agreed that he would only take three classes because he was so advanced, and the following year he went to college. At nearby Pierce College in the valley, he enrolled in classes, and I got a call from the professor, who said he had never had a student so young and he wanted to make sure fifteen-year-old Brawley didn't have an unpleasant experience. I told him that college was what Brawley was interested in, then explained more about his background and the kind of educational experiences he had had over the years.

I'd known that the traditional American educational system wasn't right for Brawley for a long time—that basic assembly line where every kid takes the same class and learns, or attempts to learn, precisely the same things. It's a system that doesn't allow young people to pursue either their long-held passions or their passing whims, but he had learned in a very unusual way and I wanted to be sure things went well for him when he went full-time into college—if, indeed, he truly wanted that.

I called the admissions departments at five or six universities and spoke with their heads of admissions, learning that at schools like Stanford, Iowa State, and others, they often preferred homeschooled students over kids who had been educated more conventionally. They didn't mean the kind of homeschooling where students took courses off the Internet; the kids they were eager to have come to their schools were those who knew *how* to investigate what they were interested in, kids who would dive in with both feet until they were saturated and ready to move on to something else that inspired them.

Brawley was gifted, and a confident self-starter, and he was now joining his father and his grandmother in being outside of the constraints of a public education. I loved imagining, as well, the life my boy would shape for himself in schools and outside of them. Yet how could I have known back then that Brawley would dive into acting like his old man and appear in five films before ultimately deciding to enter medical school?

———

It may be hard to imagine me in a wig. Indeed, my first Merchant Ivory film, shot in France in 1994, was *Jefferson in Paris,* and it was a departure for me in many ways. It was the first time I'd worn an eighteenth-century costume or portrayed one of America's founding fathers. Director James Ivory originally had wanted Christopher Reeve to play the film's leading role, but he changed his mind when Merchant Ivory created a partnership with Disney and Disney executives suggested me. Luckily, Ivory told the *New York Times,* "He seemed extremely thoughtful. He had the right personal dignity. The right age. Tall. Most of all, he's a good actor." I'm not sure about my personal dignity, but it was nice to hear he thought I was the right height.

I liked James very much as well, and, together with his partner Ismail Merchant, his filmmaking reputation was unimpeachable, so I was delighted to have the opportunity to work with him. The story the film tells begins in 1784 when Jefferson's wife, Martha, dies and he accepts an appointment as our young nation's minister to France, taking the position that had been held for nine years by Benjamin Franklin.

Jefferson sends back to America for some of his slaves, including Sally Hemings. She lives in the Jefferson household in Paris and begins a sexual relationship with the widowed Jefferson and becomes pregnant.

During my research for the role, I had traveled to the University of Virginia and spoken with history professors as well as venturing to Jefferson's home at Monticello, and everywhere people asked me, "Is this a movie about Sally Hemings?" With fingers crossed behind my back, I fibbed that no, the film would have little to do with Sally, because at the time all of us knew that their purported relationship was just a rumor.

The *New York Times* wouldn't break the news for four more years that a respected DNA study had conclusively linked Hemings's children to the descendants of Jefferson, but our script, written by Merchant and Ivory's longtime collaborator Ruth Prawer Jhabvala, nonetheless suggested that the two became intimate during their time in Paris. About halfway through the film, in fact, Sally becomes the predominant character—which I thought was appropriate.

The more I read about Jefferson, as well as his own writings, the more impressed I was by his intellect and his energy. He was a man who was extremely interested in every aspect of the world around him, and someone who was very much of the earth. He drew inspiration for the liberty of man from his deep study of the natural world around him. He was extraordinary in the truest sense of the word, and I felt privileged to portray him.

As time goes by, I find roles I play stay with me more and more. They become encoded into me. I figure the intense way I prepare in the first place makes it difficult for me to lose/shake off the character I've created after the shooting is done. Following *Jefferson in Paris*, for example, it was no accident that I had to have all my windows redone in a Jeffersonian style and a gazebo built on my Malibu property that matched Monticello's. His style had inspired me.

James Ivory remains legendary for his gentleness, his reserve, and his penchant for speaking few words. Alternately, his life and filmmaking partner Ismail, now deceased, was a bold and outgoing Indian guy. He was famous for asking casts and crews to come in on Saturdays for Indian food and dancing, and perhaps a bit of filming—his particular trick for getting more work than he was actually paying for. That recurring ploy landed Merchant Ivory at the top of a list of producers and directors we were warned *not* to work for. But everyone did so anyway—because the two men were great people, and they made fine films, and those Indian-food Saturdays were always pretty fun.

———

We shot *The Golden Bowl* in London and several lo-cations in Leicestershire and Lincolnshire, and once more I found myself in a costume drama that necessi-tated a kind of stylized acting that I generally shy away from. But I had thoroughly enjoyed my first Mer-chant Ivory experience five years before, and Brawley was with me, and the material, based on a Henry James novel, was excellent.

The picture tells the story of an extravagantly rich American widower, played by me, and his sheltered daughter—a terrific Kate Beckinsale—who separately marry, then discover that their new mates, a beauti-ful American expatriate and an impoverished Italian aristocrat, are actually in love with each other and are involved in an elaborate conspiracy of seduction and deceit.

Set in England and Italy between 1903 and 1909, *The Golden Bowl* was Merchant Ivory's third film based on a James novel. The company had developed notoriety and a devoted following for creating literary period films—winning more than thirty Academy Award nominations and six Oscars along the way. Uma Thurman, who plays the beautiful young American aristocrat my character falls in love with, is absolutely wonderful in the film. I am proud of *The Golden Bowl* because although the role is small, my character and his wealth and power are threaded through the other characters' lives, ultimately taking charge of them in ways over which they have no control.

When the film premiered at Cannes in 2000, we all were joined by Harvey Weinstein, the aggressive head of Miramax and *The Golden Bowl*'s executive producer. The Cannes committee was enthusiastic enough about the film that it had already been nominated for the Palme d'Or, and following its premiere screening the audience leapt to its feet and applauded for an incredible amount of time. At the party that followed, people were equally passionate in their reactions. When I found James among the crowd, I asked, "Have you ever had a response like this before?"

"No," he stated incredulously, and we were both enthusiastic until Harvey told us that although we had done "a good job," the film had problems. They could be fixed with a series of cuts, he assured us.

"I wouldn't know what to cut," James told him.

"Well, I do," Harvey said—then he did just that in the weeks that followed.

Weinstein had a long-standing reputation as a producer who would ruthlessly edit films directors and editors had worked painstakingly to create, so we thought we were prepared for what might become of our film. We weren't. Once Harvey and company had completed their "edit," the picture had been reduced to shreds. The filmmakers were initially crushed, then became furious with the suggested changes.

Cool-headed James eventually persuaded Harvey to sell the film back to Merchant Ivory for the $15 million it had cost to make it, but because of the rules of the industry and the academy, the film would not be eligible for consideration for the upcoming Academy Awards. Ismail and James opted simply to let it sit in the can for a year, a decision that was wise, in part, but lost us real momentum and a lot of buzz by the time the picture finally premiered in May 2001.

Kurt Vonnegut possessed a tremendous wit and knowledge of humor and storytelling. In the years between my Merchant Ivory films, I did two films based on novels by Vonnegut, long one of my favorite authors. It was a young director named Keith Gordon who first imagined me as the lead in *Mother Night*, and Vonnegut himself, I learned, was enthusiastic about my being cast in the role of Howard W. Campbell Jr., an American who moves with his family to Germany after World War I and eventually becomes a successful German-language playwright. As World War II looms, Campbell is recruited to spy for the

United States, transmitting Nazi propaganda in incendiary speeches that contain hidden messages, which can only be decoded by Allied intelligence.

Ten-year-old Brawley plays Campbell as a young man in the film, and it was great to have him as part of our team, yet *Mother Night,* in the end, was one of only three feature films in which he appeared before he concluded that show business just isn't his deal—a decision that was just fine by me.

When I asked Vonnegut why he ended up writing a World War II spy story, he said it was because he was in Dresden when it was virtually destroyed by Allied bombs. He was in the town, way underground hiding out in a meat locker, and just got lucky he didn't get burned to death. Before the bombing, he told me, "I would go to cocktail parties and people would talk about spies, but nobody knew shit about spies. And it just caught my fancy that a spy could be right in front of me in that room—and be successful and a playwright, someone who got tweaked into all of this through his art."

That very thing happens to playwrights, actors, artists, too. When you think you're telling the greatest story ever told, you're often right on the edge of becoming a complete liar, because your story is only as good as the moment it's told in. You may get caught in your own act.

As Vonnegut wrote in a foreword to a later edition of the novel, "We are what we pretend to be, so we must be careful about what we pretend to be."

I was incredibly nervous about my role before we began to shoot. That used to happen to me a lot, but in *Mother Night* I would have to face a camera dressed in a Nazi uniform and spew horrible rhetoric about Jews—and it wasn't an easy thing to do, even though it was only acting. I stayed up all night for five days and was drunk and hungover and really a wreck, but I finally pulled it all together. I think my internal anguish helped me play Campbell convincingly—as a guy who gets even Joseph Goebbels to believe he is as vile as the worst of the Nazis, all while passing vital intelligence to the West.

When I saw *Mother Night* for the first time, I was in Montreal and Vonnegut was with me. It's a very unusual picture, and at its conclusion the audience was just kind of stunned. No one was quite sure what to make of what the movie meant to be or to say. As we got into our limo following the screening, Kurt asked me, "They were perturbed, weren't they?" I told him I thought the film perturbed the hell out of them.

"Great. That's great," he responded. "That's what you want. I could give a shit about whether they liked it or not. But that it perturbed them, that's what you want."

The film received generally good reviews, and a few reviewers thought it was a singular and altogether extraordinary picture. But the studio stopped running ads a week after the film opened, preferring to put their eggs into the basket of another film they were releasing, *Shine* with Geoffrey Rush. I knew we were sunk. I asked the studio, "Please treat us with respect and don't drop us in the ads." But they did. So I called the *New York Times* and the *Los Angeles Times* to see how much a quarter-page weekend ad would cost, and I think it was about $50,000 at the time—a price I told one of the studio heads I was willing to pay. He read me the riot act. "You can't take out ads!" he shouted, claiming it was simply a mistake that they had been dropped. He assured me the ads would begin again, but he was openly lying. That's what the film industry is about. You make some, you lose some—it's a gamble.

In the film adaptation of Vonnegut's novel *Breakfast of Champions,* which we shot three years later, I play a cross-dressing used-car-lot manager—a part that was just the tiniest bit against type and a role I was eager to take on. I told the film's costumer that I wanted a dress that felt very sensual, the kind of thing men just don't ever get to wear, silky and sexy. Together we came up with a sheer little red dress with straps that was big enough for me, but it wasn't quite right until I turned it around and wore it backward so my nipples were exposed and I looked like a bare-breasted Phoenician woman—something I felt was key to my character Harry Le Sabre.

I was dating comedienne and actress Vicki Lewis at the time, and Vicki was playing my wife, Grace, in the film as well. When I wore heels, my tits were right at her mouth, and she loved to go, "Nom, nom, nom," like she was nursing. It was just ludicrous! Bizarre! Oh God, I had great fun doing it. And the legendary English actor Albert Finney was wonderful, too, playing the little-known science-fiction author Kilgore Trout.

After our first day of shooting, Albert suggested that we go for a drink. I said sure, but I told him I could only have one drink. He didn't like the sound of that and said, "Oh, that's going to be a real pisser," but I told him to be patient. After about an hour or so of joking around, we had drunk several bottles of wine, and I asked, "Albert, how many glasses of wine have I had?"

He looked at my glass and said, "Only one. You've never been empty."

"Yeah. That's what I meant!" I told him.

Bruce Willis plays the film's lead as car-lot owner Dwayne Hoover, and I thought he was terrifically funny. We were directed by Alan Rudolph, whom I had worked for in his earlier film *Afterglow*. Alan wrote the screenplay, but many people felt it unfairly turned the dark satire of Vonnegut's namesake novel into slapstick humor. *Entertainment Weekly* gave the film an F rating and claimed that "Rudolph, in an act of insane folly, seems to think that what matters is the story. The result . . . is a movie so unhinged it practically dares you not to hate it."

Hate it? Well, we certainly had a ton of fun making it. And any time I had the pleasure to work with Finney and Rudolph and Vonnegut was time well spent in my book.

I had met the little redheaded Vicki Lewis while we were filming the James L. Brooks comedy *I'll Do Anything* five years before. She and I laughed a lot together and she joined me at my place near Zuma Beach in Malibu, where we lived for a number of years. We never considered marriage, in large part because she preferred to be involved in at least two relationships at the same time. Truly. It was an imperative for her; she couldn't help it. And one of her men at any moment *had* to be a comedy writer—because she was always in need of material. An actor like me was a fine choice for fellow number two because I could help her get publicity when we appeared out together.

I understood Vicki's needs, and accepted them, and thought she was great, although her domestic necessities sometimes created real chaos. Vicki had been part of the cast of the hit television series *NewsRadio,* and when its star Phil Hartman was shot and killed by his wife, the entire cast was devastated. The intensity of cocreating a show at such a high comedic level had generated great stress among the group, and everyone was already in danger of burning out. When they lost Phil so suddenly and tragically, things hit a breaking point.

Vicki's costar Andy Dick had a son who was about seven years old, and he hadn't seen his father in several weeks because of the show's hectic schedule. He wasn't going to school and couldn't read yet, and Vicki was very concerned about his welfare. She brought him out to Malibu to stay with us, and the boy began to work with Brawley's tutor each day. He was here for a couple of months before *NewsRadio* was finally canceled, and following the cancellation, Andy was able to devote the time to his son that the boy desperately needed.

Vicki was wonderful to children and friends who

were in need, and our relationship flourished, too, for most of a decade. It was a time during which I became very interested in the state of my health and the ways in which I could get back into shape. I hadn't been good to my body for many years, and it was time to show it some TLC.

It was during the filming of *Lorenzo's Oil* back in 1992 that I first began to explore alternative approaches to health and wellness. That film was based on the true story of parents whose selflessness led them to discover an herbal cure for their son Lorenzo, who suffered from adrenoleukodystrophy, a degenerative nerve disorder. Little Lorenzo's real parents and several consultants on the film were responsible for opening my eyes to what was unfolding in the alternative medical world.

Then, when I was making the Oliver Stone film *U Turn* five years later, I met an anti-aging physician who introduced me to hormone imbalances and replacement strategies, immune system function, and the possibility of using human growth hormone therapy as a way to stay youthful and full of energy. And so, I went with him on a journey.

Under this doctor's care, I began injecting HGH into my stomach every day and getting impressive results. A man's natural production of HGH begins to fall off as early as eighteen or so, and by the time you're middle-aged, its dramatically lower levels begin to cause all kinds of problems. But with the use of HGH injections, I discovered, your testosterone levels rise, fat falls away, and your body begins to repair itself.

It was enormously expensive therapy—two or three thousand dollars a month—but it was worth it, and I remember the doctor telling me, "After a year's use, you'll be wondering why you're sticking this needle in your stomach every night, because you won't remember the way you used to look and feel. But if you stop for a couple of weeks, you'll start to feel *ugh, ugh*— you'll see and you'll feel your body start to fall apart again." And he was right.

Next, I connected with Norman Cromwell in Los Angeles, a reclusive guy who was a leader in the city's underground medical community—someone who was successfully using ozone therapy as a way to detox the body. I met Dr. Eric Braverman, a New York City physician whose focus is brain health, at an antiaging conference and I was immediately impressed by the work he was doing as well. At his PATH—Place for Achieving Total Health—Foundation, his research included models for weight control, modulating addictive behavior, early detection of Alzheimer's disease, hormone replacement therapy, and a form of brain mapping he labeled BEAM, the brain electrical assessment method.

I became such a committed patient over time that Dr. Braverman quipped that I was probably the most studied person on earth. With BEAM and additional diagnostic tools, he studied my concentration and memory; he used positron emission tomography, PET scanning, to hunt for minuscule tumors and diseases throughout my body; DXA scans to check for loss of bone density; and a brain SPECT scan, a nuclear imaging procedure designed to diagnose Alzheimer's and other neurodegenerative diseases, and to evaluate memory loss. Whew.

When all the results were in, he concluded that I had the brain of a man who would battle with addictive behavior all his life, and that my brain was physiologically predisposed to fundamental anxieties that trigger stress-induced behavior, including alcohol consumption. For virtually all of my adult life, I had endeavored to figure myself out, to better understand what I was made of and how and why I interacted with the world around me in the ways I did. I long had searched for my essence, so to speak, so it wasn't surprising that I wanted to learn as much as I could about my physical body as well. It told my real story better than any I could concoct. Soon I became a student of health and read everything I could from scientific journals, especially European journals, which seem to be way ahead of their time.

During those years I was regarded as "Nick the weirdo," because I would constantly look at blood under the dark-field microscope in my bedroom, whether it was my blood or Brawley's blood. I projected the image on a high-definition screen on the wall. The longer I spent looking at our blood, the more I realized it's another universe. It's vibrant. And the longer I studied the blood, the more humbled I was by the intricacies of life. The inner world and the outer are separated by the thinnest veneer of a façade.

What I learned during that time confirmed essential truths I already knew—that something inside me couldn't be entirely at ease in the world, couldn't find the peace I had always wanted. Yet adding a medical overlay to my introspection allowed me to relax and accept myself in new ways. My physiology dramatically affected my behavior, I learned—and it also gave me a new determination to take control of my life. I chose to continue to inject HGH; to supplement my nutrition with vitamins, hormones, ozone, and other modalities; and to be "Nick the weirdo."

Chapter 15
Fathers and Mothers

Just as my parents had long predicted, they ended their marriage after their children were grown. My mother remained in Phoenix, where she ultimately opened an antiques shop. Mom and Dad remained friends even though they no longer wanted to live under the same roof, and my father moved back to the Midwest, remaining in the irrigation-equipment business until he retired. Circulatory problems led to his having a leg amputated, then in 1978 he was hospitalized in Denver, suffering from cancer.

I received a call from my mother at my ranch near Agoura, telling me that she had heard from Dad and had spoken with his doctors. It was time. I dropped everything, drove to Phoenix, and collected her, and we continued on, driving like crazy to Denver. At the hospital, we found my sister, Nancy, who was crying as she shared the news with us that Dad had died not long before our arrival. In his room, they had packed his small suitcase and on top of it lay the wooden leg he had used since his amputation.

I was desperate to get the hell out of that hospital as soon as we could, and off we went to an unappealing motor hotel on Colfax Avenue, where I began to sob uncontrollably once I was alone in my room. My tears didn't flow because of the loss of Franklin Arthur Nolte as much as they were caused by the weight of our relationship. The connection I had to my father was peeling off, and it hurt. When I was done with the process, I was lighter; it was as if I could float. We don't know how heavy our relationships are. They are very heavy; they carry a lot of energy. With that release, I felt suddenly different and everything seemed okay—except that I couldn't stay in that dreary place.

I found where my mother and sister were staying and proposed that we hit the road. Santa Fe was only six hours south, and it was a great town, and I insisted we needed to respond to Dad's death by having some fun. Mom and Nancy quickly agreed and off we went.

In Santa Fe, we checked into the La Fonda hotel on the corner of the plaza and I was ready for a drink.

"You're going to drink on the day your father died?" my mother asked, and I told her I sure as hell was. Nancy said she wanted to join me, and the two of us adjourned to the hotel's bar, then about five minutes later, Mom joined us as well.

The three of us drank for a while by ourselves before we inevitably began to make some new friends. We partied until the bar closed, then invited folks upstairs to continue the good time. But one by one, our new friends would curiously inquire about the prosthesis lying on the mantel. "Oh, that's our dad's wooden leg," I would tell them. "He died today."

The explanation inevitably sent them packing. We partied for several days at the La Fonda, and somehow it seemed to be the right thing to do. Lank would have been happy to have the three people in the world to whom he was closest send him off in such a way, I suggested to Mom and Nance, and they agreed.

Early in the 1990s, I had gotten a call from screenwriter and director Paul Schrader. He had written *Taxi Driver* and *Raging Bull,* both directed by Martin Scorsese, and was directing his own films by now, and he wanted to know if I was interested in reading the script he'd written based on Russell Banks's much-lauded novel *Affliction.*

I was blown away by the power of the screenplay Paul had crafted, then I read Russell's novel as well, and I eagerly told Paul I was all in. I said I would love to play the film's lead, small-town cop Wade White-house, but I would need to wait a couple of years. I just wasn't ready to play the part yet, I explained.

Paul was floored. What in the hell was I talking about? It had taken him years to raise the $6 million he needed to make the film, and we both agreed that there likely wasn't anyone other than me who was so suited to playing Wade.

"Listen," I said, trying to explain, "there's something in Russell's book that is beyond me right now. I don't fully understand it, and it's going to be vital for me to understand it if I'm going to do the part justice. It seems to me like the affliction is universal to all men. We're all afflicted."

Paul knew what I meant, of course. The affliction we all suffer from is that for thousands of years, fathers have failed to teach their sons how to love. Our fathers should teach us how to love as men, yet they do not. Wade, the desperately lonely and lost character I would play, powerfully *wants* to love his daughter and his ex-wife, but he just doesn't know how. It's a tricky theme that I don't think had been explored before Russell explored it in *Affliction*. If I was going to portray Wade,

I knew I would have to deeply mine his predicament before I could truly *become* him.

My own father had suffered a mysterious but terribly debilitating emotional wound in the South Pacific during World War II. I didn't know who he was when he returned home at the end of the war, and although he and I never fought during the years that followed, I didn't see much of him and I never truly got to know him, never knew what it was that he cared about the most. He was a closed book.

As I began my preparation to play Wade Whitehouse, I knew I needed to consider my relationship with my late father as a piece of that process. I longed for part of him and thought about that old wooden leg. Yet when I looked for it, I couldn't find it, so I called Nancy, certain that she would have it. But she didn't. Mom had it, we agreed, but when I called her, she told me she was sure that Nancy was safeguarding it back east. I explained that Nancy was certain she *didn't* have it, then I couldn't help but start to laugh. The only possibility now seemed to be that we had inadvertently left Dad's leg at the hotel in Santa Fe.

By the time I felt emotionally ready to play Wade, I had become intrigued by the idea that Paul Newman would be perfect in the part of Wade Whitehouse's alcoholic and abusive father, Glen. I approached him, and Paul was kind enough to read the script and say good things about it and the film we planned to make, but he replied in an interesting way as he turned my offer down. "I don't think my audience would accept me in that role," he said, and it took a bit for me to understand what he meant. Paul knew his on-screen persona was too good-looking, romantic, and principled to portray someone as destroyed by living as Glen is. The film would suffer, in other words, if Paul Newman appeared in it—at least as far as Paul Newman was concerned.

So, next I approached James Coburn, another actor I greatly admired. Jimmy, born in Nebraska like me, suffered terribly from rheumatoid arthritis and hadn't appeared in many films in recent years, yet he had begun to use something called MSM, methylsulfonyl-methane, a sulfur compound available at most health food stores. The result was amazing, he claimed, and although it didn't cure his arthritis, it did relieve his pain, allowing him to move more freely and ultimately say yes to the dark and complex character of Glen Whitehouse.

Then I called Sissy Spacek and said, "Sissy, I've got a role for you. It's not a big role, but it's a vital role."

She responded in her Southern twang, "Niiiick, I'm retired." I said, "Sissy, you can't retire."

"Well, they don't send me scripts," she explained.

"Well, I'm sending you a script," I told her. "And it's based on a novel by a well-known writer. And there is a pivotal scene that tells the audience about the whole tragedy of the story when the woman—you—realizes that her man doesn't know how to love. The woman sees his masculine violence and she rejects it. She totally rejects this idea that violence makes the world go 'round. Because it doesn't. Violence stops the world."

That was all Sissy needed to hear, and she was in. Paul Schrader was the perfect director for this difficult material. Russell Banks himself drove me around impoverished rural New England, pointing out his old haunts and the places he re-created as he brought Wade and his story to life on the page. He helped me understand that Wade doesn't believe he's insane, and so neither could the audience. The insanity is simply Wade's denial of his utterly trapped circumstances.

Affliction premiered in February 1999 to strong critical praise, and Janet Maslin in the *New York Times* wrote that I gave the performance of my career. The *San Francisco Chronicle*'s critic Edward Guthmann agreed that I had "never been better. Nolte has played angry blue-collar men like Wade before, but never so heartbreakingly and never in material as deeply felt."

By the time the film was completed, I already knew that Wade was one of my favorite roles ever. I had mustered something deep inside me in order to portray the rage and violence that is primary to Wade's character—a capacity for violence that's in us all, but which very few of us ever confront. By the time *Affliction* was in theaters and gaining a small but very enthusiastic following, I had successfully come to terms with who Wade is and how he is afflicted by his father, but I couldn't be sure I knew my own father or understood my relationship with him any better than before making the film. Lank Nolte remained something of a mystery to me—despite the depth of my feelings for him.

I received my second Academy Award nomination for best actor for *Affliction* and was nominated for a Golden Globe as well. I won in the best-actor category at the awards presented by the New York Film Critics Circle and the National Society of Film Critics, but on the night of the Academy Awards, the smart money was probably on Tom Hanks's winning for his performance in *Saving Private Ryan*. I was seated beside James Coburn at the ceremony, and very early in the proceedings, Jimmy won as best supporting actor, being selected over heavyweight actors like Robert Duvall, Ed Harris, Geoffrey Rush, and Billy Bob Thornton, and I was delighted for him. His work in *Affliction* had been astounding.

A few moments later, I received a call on my cell phone during a television commercial break. It was my friend Alan Rudolph, who had directed me in both *Afterglow* and *Breakfast of Champions* and who is one of the most deviously fun guys in the business. Alan simply wanted me to know that in the history of the Academy Awards, "no lead actor has ever won if the costar wins."

"Oh, shit," I whispered to him as the commercial break ended, and I chuckled with resignation. And sure enough, near the end of the evening Sophia Loren announced that Italian actor-director Roberto Benigni had won the best-actor Oscar for *Life Is Beautiful*—and that was that.

When word got out that director Terrence Malick planned to make a new film for the first time in nearly two decades, the buzz among A-list actors was immediate and loud. Everyone in town wanted a role in the new picture, which would be based on James Jones's World War II novel *The Thin Red Line*. Ironically, I was preparing at the time for a film in which I would play the part of James Jones himself. Also, I was a lot older than most of the guys who were determined to be cast by Terry, and that was a worry to both Terry and me.

Over the course of four separate lunches together, Terry and I mulled over whether the film had a role I was right for. He considered the possibility of creating an entirely new character—a general far away from the battlefield—but neither of us ever became enthusiastic about that approach for bringing me into the project. As we ate, we talked as much about philosophy, poetry, and even birds as we did about the picture. Terry's meanderings were always captivating, and he was an excellent listener. During our fourth lunch, he announced that he'd changed his mind. Yes, I was older than the other actors he had cast, but I *would* play Lieutenant Colonel Gordon Tall, and he knew I would play the hell out of the role, he told me. I was elated.

I was scheduled to arrive on location in Port Douglas, Queensland, Australia, several weeks after shooting commenced, and while I was at home preparing for the role of Colonel Tall, I received a note from Terry that simply said, "Self will run riot." As part of my turn toward bringing my body back to optimal health via a variety of alternative medical therapies and supplementation, I also had quit drinking and doing cocaine and had started regularly attending Alcoholics Anonymous meetings. So I was quite familiar with the phrase, pulled from a quote by AA founder Bill Wilson, who wrote, "The alcoholic is an extreme example of self will run riot, though he usually doesn't think so." Alcoholics and control junkies want to have power over the world around them. They're selfish and will do anything they can, knowingly or not, to get what they want from people and life. So it's a problem that can manifest in self-destruction.

Colonel Tall is a man who puts himself in jeopardy repeatedly, regardless of how the world is exploding around him, determined to impose his self-will on the course of history no matter the cost. It was a brilliant note from a director whose talent was enormous—and I took it to heart.

When I reached the set in Australia, I was greeted by some uneasy actors. No one was sure who was the central character in the story, and several guys were determined to make themselves the lead. And they were bothered, too, by the way in which Malick would repeatedly stop shooting three-quarters of the way through a scene, then mutter about getting back to it later. The idea of picking up a performance at an unspecified date in the future had some of the boys doubting their abilities *and* Terry's approach.

The grumblings were growing so loud that Terry agreed to schedule a cast meeting, one at which he listened carefully as, one by one, actors articulated their dismay at his disorienting directorial style. Some warned of uneven performances, begging him for a schedule that gave them a reasonable shot at emotional continuity. After patiently hearing them out, he responded, saying, "You know what, guys, you're right. So, let's go do it!"

Everyone in the room was dumbfounded. Terry managed to take the air out of the uproar without giving an inch. He listened to his cast's many complaints, told them they were right, then went on directing just as he had before. Brilliant.

Early on, one of the constant conversations among cast and crew was the war of one-upmanship between Woody Harrelson and Sean Penn. First, Woody threw a snake into Sean's trailer, then Sean retaliated by calling a local radio station, posing as Woody's assistant, and promising that Woody would appear at a local park, offering signed photographs for ten bucks apiece. Woody was furious about the setup but showed up at the park anyway and gave away autographs for free.

I had met Woody briefly once before, and one morning he called me, saying, "I really need your help. I need to get Sean to go to a certain place at a certain time. And if I suggest it, he'll know I'm up to something. Would you do this?"

I asked, "We're not going to hurt him, are we?" And Woody swore that absolutely not, no one would be injured in any way, so I said sure, I was in.

Early on a Saturday evening, Woody phoned again and asked me to come down to the police station. Port Douglas was just a one-street town with restaurants and bars on both sides, and dirt roads leading out into the jungles of northern Australia. It's a rough little frontier town, and it's beautiful. The police station is simply a small beach bungalow, and Woody met me at the entrance with a devilish grin, then led me down a hall to a back room.

"Should we use a gun?" he conspiratorially asked a policeman in the room, who was filling a handgun with blanks. I couldn't imagine what Woody had promised them in order to bring the cops on board, but before I could find out, it was time for me to play my little role. Woody coached me to telephone Sean, telling him I had been in a minor fender bender, explaining that it wasn't my fault, but that I had to undergo a blood-alcohol test because I was a foreigner. I needed Sean to vouch for me in person with the cops, I told him, and he fell for it.

It was such an elaborately planned gag that Woody had three officers working with him: two in uniform, and one dressed as the tough guy who had caused the car accident. He was a rough-looking Aussie, covered in tattoos, and he and everyone else delivered Oscar-worthy performances.

Sean arrived and was directed to the back room. There, he joined one officer, the phony criminal, and me. The policeman told Sean the circumstances were only a formality and not to worry. All Sean needed to do was verify my identity while we waited on the results of a blood-alcohol test. Sean looked worriedly in my direction, but I shook my head. No, I hadn't been drinking.

Soon, the policemen who had been at the front desk entered and escorted the tough guy from the room. As they made their way down the hall, we could hear a vicious verbal confrontation. The officer still in the room sprang up and took off toward the terrible ruckus, his gun drawn. Things got even louder and more intense, and Sean, being Sean, crept out into the hallway to sneak a peek.

Boom! Boom! Suddenly two gunshots echoed loudly,

and Sean came hauling ass back into the room and ran to the back door, trying to get out. But it was locked, so he tried the windows, and they were locked. At that moment, the tattooed guy rushed in, shouting, "I'm getting the fuck out of here, motherfucker! And I'm going to kill somebody if I have to! You, you're going to drive me out of here!"

Sean had fallen to the floor but now he cautiously stood, saying with all the control he could muster, "No reason to shoot. I'm going to take you wherever you want to go. Don't shoot anybody."

One of the cops nervously said, "The keys . . . on the desk," and Sean took them, unlocked the back door, opened it—and there was Woody with his camera in his hands. He shot a quick photograph of Sean—still scared out of his wits—then pointed at two video cameras that were recording the scene, and began to chant, "I am king! I am king!"

It was a great gag, maybe the best gag I'd ever seen. How Woody ever convinced the cops to help him pull it off, I don't know. It was just crazy. Sean most definitely did *not* laugh, yet he was enormously relieved that the situation had not been real. All he could say was, "You know, if I had been in L.A., I would have had my gun, and somebody would have been killed." He was completely freaked out.

Woody left town for a bit soon thereafter, but before he did everyone on the set kept an eager eye on what kind of retribution Sean would exact. Nothing had occurred before he left, but his children remained in town. Woody was a strict vegan, and his kids had never eaten meat in their lives, so when he returned he was knocked over by the news that they *loved* the delicious beef soup they lately were being served each day. Woody was *really* pissed off.

Woody's eyes emit a mad intensity, even when he's relaxed. I would *never* fuck with him, ever. And apparently, he was headed directly for Sean with a murderous look when Terry's wife, Ecky, intervened. Without knowing about the kids' dietary restrictions, she confessed to having been feeding them a steady supply of ham sandwiches the whole time they had been in Port Douglas—so the beef soup wasn't the half of it! Her confession at least momentarily blunted Woody's anger and allowed him to regain some self-control. Sean stopped needling him, and the two settled into an edgy truce—because it was time to get serious.

As our shoot progressed, Terry continued to stop filming scenes before they were finished—the very thing he had assured his actors he would stop doing. He would shoot the spine of the scene, the beginning and middle, but not the end—and this happened time after time. And virtually every day, he would do something curious, too. When only a couple of hours of daylight were left and the light had grown soft and rich and full—"golden light," as it is known in the industry—Terry would stop whatever scene we were shooting and want to revisit one of the unfinished scenes. He wasn't concerned about his actors' performance continuities, or that the light that closed a scene would be very different from the light in its opening, or even that the earlier footage was shot in another location—which naturally drove cinematographer John Toll totally crazy.

I was paying close attention to how all of this was playing out, and finally I was sure I understood what Terry was trying to do. He wanted as many scenes as possible to end in "golden light," regardless of the discontinuity. This was time and cost prohibitive, and may have gotten him fired from the film had the studio heads gotten wind of his intention and the reason for his secrecy.

I told Terry that I was onto him. But I assured him I believed in his methods and his track record as a director, and, in turn, he revealed some of his reasoning. He explained that he wanted to go beyond a conventional writer's concept of how you made a film, beyond the conventional director's vision, beyond what was normally done by everyone in front of or behind the camera. His goal, he said, was to get all of us to let go of the choices we made as we prepared and simply face the unknown. He didn't want his actors, for example, to search for a particular emotion they had established a day or a week ago. He only wanted us to move toward the discovery of new truths. I suggested he must be seeking divine inspiration, and he agreed with a mischievous grin.

My character, Colonel Gordon Tall, had been imagined by James Jones as a West Point graduate who'd come of age at a time when the concept of the noble warrior had become outdated but not yet extinct. Before World War II, Tall was overwhelmed by the fear of an empty destiny—a fear so total that by the time the Battle of Guadalcanal occurred, he had completely lost sight of the war's objective, replacing it with nothing more than a personal obsession. The men under his command were simply pawns in his own selfish drama.

Tall's antagonist, Captain Bugger Staros, played by Elias Koteas, makes an argument for saving the lives of his men and refuses Tall's orders for a direct frontal assault on a hill they are attempting to capture. Staros will not simply sacrifice his men for the sake of a hollow objective. But the Japanese resistance weakens in the face of the company's heavy assault, and with terrible loss of life on both sides, the battle is won. Tall revels in his achievement and basks in his ownership of the hilltop.

However, as he comes down from the hill, soaking in his moment of imagined glory, his eyes can't avoid the severed and mutilated bodies of soldiers strewn all over God's garden. He sees the carnage he alone has created, and Tall is devastated, breaking down under the weight of his own reckoning, and is perhaps a little redeemed by the emergence of his own humanity.

It's very powerful stuff—a profound challenge and the very reason why this work has always compelled me in the way it has. But that said, I had as much fun inside the character of Gordon Tall as any I ever played. Terry and I established a rhythm that was exhilarating. He would come up with new lines in the middle of a scene and yell them out to me. Some days, he'd drop five pages of poetry on me or throw out Latin phrases. He didn't want us to learn our lines by rote; put in your words, they just might catch fire. The entire process was a gas—and a highlight of my professional life.

I was struck as we made the picture that—in their separate media of book and film—James Jones and Terrence Malick essentially created a love story. In a dilemma that is virtually incomprehensible for most of us, a combat soldier uses his rifle to try to kill the people who are hell-bent on killing him. In those moments, you create a bond with your comrade fighting beside you that is the most profound kind of love humans can experience. You do your best to keep your buddy alive, and he strives to keep *you* from being killed, and each of you is willing to die to protect the other. As far as Jones and Malick were concerned, there simply is no other love that's more powerful, more fully etched with life's great meaning. It is the *only* meaning-filled thing that war offers us. And its beauty is almost entirely obscured by the fact that war also destroys everything it touches.

I often wished while I was making *The Thin Red Line* that at long last I could talk with my late father about the war. It was something he never wanted to discuss, so perhaps even in my middle age there would have been almost nothing he would have been willing to share. He and his contemporaries certainly had reason to be circumspect, if not entirely silent. Virtually each one of them had had to deal with horrific experiences. Many of them also came home killers, and they did not want to be killers. They didn't talk to their sons, didn't talk to anyone—even among themselves—because what could possibly be said about the inhumanity of which they had been a part?

_____

The Thin Red Line was nominated for seven Academy Awards in 1999, including best picture and best director. None of us from the big ensemble cast received an acting nomination, which was surprising, yet we all were thrilled that Terry received the recognition he deserved after a twenty-year hiatus away from making films. And perhaps more than anything, it seemed wonderfully fitting that the film won the Golden Bear, the highest prize awarded at the Berlin International Film Festival.

My mother's health had begun to decline significantly by the time *The Thin Red Line* premiered, and I doubt she saw the film. Over the years, she had paid attention to my career, and she enjoyed watching me act on-screen. She claimed she had always known that I would be successful at whatever endeavors I pursued, but my celebrity certainly didn't mean much to her. She thought it was fun, but she had no interest at all in joining me at premieres or award ceremonies, and she'd never been someone who vicariously reveled in her son's accomplishments.

My mother had remained in Phoenix during her last decades. She and her good friend Helen Buda had operated an antiques store called the Little House, and it was well-known and very successful. Neither of them had a background in antique furniture, but both women had great taste. I always enjoyed going to auctions with my mom. It was uncanny, I thought, how she always knew what would sell and what wouldn't, and what was real and what was not. She was a natural.

Yet Mom had a tough time with old age, largely because she had so much pride. She wouldn't fly anywhere because that meant negotiating her way through airports. She couldn't walk far and she refused to be seen in a wheelchair, even briefly. She became so reclusive that when Brawley and his cousin, Nancy's son, Eric, would drive over from California to see her, she wouldn't open her door for them. She began to tell Nancy and me often that she loved us—something she had seldom done over the decades—but when Nancy asked her to move in with her, Mom immediately rebuffed her and wouldn't speak of the possibility again. No parent should be a burden to their children, she explained.

When I learned in September 2000 that she was failing dramatically and wouldn't live much longer, I responded to the news by doing something crazy—blowing out my calf and the plantar fascia in my foot by trying to move a four-thousand-pound machine as I leaned into it on my toes. *Bullooom!* My leg was instantly torn apart. That white light people report as death approaches? I saw that light and it knocked me flat out. I woke up six hours later. I know I did it intentionally. I was running from the loss.

I was recuperating at Saint John's Health Center in Santa Monica when I received a call from Mom on a Monday, asking me how soon I could be in Phoenix. When I told her I could get there by Friday, she said, "That long?" then hung up. Her time had come.

Matt Tromans, once Brawley's tutor, had become my assistant and was visiting my hospital room as I briefly spoke to my mother, and as soon as I put the phone down, I told him, "We can't wait 'til they release me Friday, I've got to get to Phoenix. Now." Matt collected my clothes, my meds, and some crutches, and we snuck out of the hospital.

I had been observing closely as my mother steadily declined for a number of years, but I was caught totally off guard by the state in which I found her at her house in Phoenix about six hours later. Toothless and frail, she seemed to be caving in on herself. She was clutching her jutting collarbones and her pain was visibly intense, yet she continued to live despite suffering from pneumonia and gangrene in her right leg. This was the same leg I'd injured. Coincidence or something deeper? It was impossible not to mull over the connection.

Nancy had been by her side until she was forced back east to deal with a household emergency for a few days, so I was alone. I sat down next to my mother's bed, stroked her hair, and whispered that everything would be okay. She heard my voice, opened her eyes, and said, "Oh, you!" Hilariously dark to the end, she simultaneously scowled and pleaded for some form of pain alleviation.

Because of my injuries, I had traveled to Arizona with a wide array of pharmaceuticals, and it was fortunate that I had them with me. I crushed several tablets of OxyContin, morphine, and Lorcet, then stirred the powder into a glass of vodka, orange juice, and cranberry juice. I topped it off with a drop of GHB, a relaxant and analgesic I had discovered about the time I quit drinking and that, to my mind, was the best painkiller yet known to humankind.

My makeshift concoction hit the spot. Soon after beginning to sip it, Mom nodded her head in silent approval and her hands released their death grip on her collarbones. Matt and I made sure that some of this special cocktail was always at her bedside. We spent most of the next three days doing what little we could to make her comfortable. She and I virtually never spoke, choosing not to talk about the lifetime of memories and shared experiences that hung in the air, letting the silence be the thing that connected us.

On Friday, five days after Matt and I had arrived, I sensed that it was time to do something else, something I thought might subtly lend her a hand. I bent over and kissed her cheek, then told her that I needed to step out for just a bit. "Don't worry though," I added. "Do whatever you need to do while I'm gone." When I walked back into her bedroom fifteen minutes later, my iconoclastic mother, Helen King Nolte, had left the building.

Chapter 16
H, GHB, and the PCH

When I first met playwright and actor Sam Shepard, he didn't like me and I didn't much like him. I had just made Martin Scorsese's *Cape Fear,* in which Sam's longtime life partner Jessica Lange played my wife. She and I always got along beautifully and she's a wonderful actor. Sam, who had accompanied her to an event honoring Scorsese and Robert De Niro, was already well oiled when I walked up to say hello to the two of them. He promptly announced that *Cape Fear* was a "horseshit Hollywood film." The remark made Jessica uncomfortable, I could tell, so I attempted some small talk by asking him, "How's your farm?" He dismissively turned to Jessica, saying, "Did you hear this idiot? How's your farm, he wants to know." Then he turned back to me and said, "I live on a *ranch,* asshole."

Honestly, I was only vaguely aware of who Sam was at that point, which probably had something to do with the competitive jealousy of contemporaries, but I had paid little attention to American theater since I'd left it in the early seventies. Even then, I ignorantly assumed that there hadn't been any American playwrights worth a second look since the heyday of Tennessee Williams, Arthur Miller, and William Inge. But, boy, was I wrong.

It was Albert Finney who introduced Sam and me professionally, so to speak. Albert and I had worked together on *Breakfast of Champions*, and a couple months following that shoot, he sent me a script called *Simpatico*, written by Sam Shepard. I liked it, agreed to take part in the project, and felt like I should bone up on Shepard's writing. I soon read everything he had written. I was floored. If he isn't the best American playwright of the second half of the twentieth century, I don't know who is.

Sam believes theater is a superior art form to film— full stop. Over time I changed my mind entirely about the man, his talents, and his artistic integrity. When, not long before my mother's death, Sam contacted me to see if I would be interested in joining my friends Sean Penn and Woody Harrelson—their feud long settled by now—onstage in the San Francisco world premiere of Sam's play *The Late Henry Moss*, I jumped at the chance.

But in September 2000, my beloved mother had just died, I'd terribly injured my leg and foot, and I'd come down with pneumonia during the few days I spent at my mother's bedside. I was a physical and emotional wreck. I sent my assistant Matt back to California and I checked into Phoenix's Arizona Biltmore Hotel, where I slept for about thirty hours without waking. My sister, Nancy, repeatedly tried to reach me by phone from New Jersey, and when she couldn't she finally convinced the hotel's manager to open the door to my room to see if I was alive.

I was, it turned out, but I was in bad enough shape that I was immediately transferred to a Scottsdale hospital, where I slowly began to recover. On a Thursday, still less than a week after Mom's death, I remembered that I was scheduled to be in San Francisco the following Monday to begin rehearsals for Sam's play—something that seemed virtually impossible, given my condition. I reached Sam by telephone and tried to explain.

"Sam, my mother died. I'm in the hospital with walking pneumonia. And that's goofy, because I can't move without a walking cast because my leg is busted up," I explained. But before I could say more, Sam shot back without sympathy, "My mother has died. I've had pneumonia. Let's pretend none of that happened. And we'll see you in San Francisco on Monday." Then he hung up.

I still don't know how I managed it, but grieving, sick, and hobbled, I presented myself at a read-through of the play at the Theatre on the Square in San Francisco four days later. An incredible cast had been assembled, including my old buddies Sean Penn and Woody Harrelson, and James Gammon. Gammon was a legendary stage and film actor who had directed me in my *last* theater performance, in *Picnic,* almost thirty years before.

The Theatre on the Square in San Francisco was the venue where we would perform, but the production was staged by the Magic Theatre, the company where Sam got his start as playwright-in-residence back in the 1970s and where his Pulitzer Prize–winning play *Buried Child* was first performed. He was returning to the Bay Area after a long absence to stage *The Late Henry Moss* for the first time, and Sam's reputation plus the quality of the cast he had assembled had created real buzz. We would play for only a six-week limited run, yet well before we opened people were already hocking tickets for two and three thousand dollars apiece.

Set in Shepard's mythic American West, *Henry*

Moss is the story of two brothers who return home to confront each other, their violent past, and the death of their father, Henry Moss, played by Gammon, for whom Shepard had written the role of the deceased father who is, despite his death, a constant presence on-stage.

After an early workshop production in New York, Shepard had looked for a home for a full production of the play, and the theater where his career truly took off made perfect sense. He approached Sean, who lives in nearby Marin County, and he was quickly on board because, in part, doing the play would allow him to work near home. Sean suggested me as the elder Moss brother and his rival. Sam liked the idea; by then, I had appeared in the film version of Shepard's *Simpatico*, and he liked my work in it and apparently no longer thought of me as an asshole. It took no time at all for the two men to reel me in.

Sean and Woody had well and truly buried the hatchet by then, and Sean encouraged Woody, who lives in Hawaii, to call Sam about a small role that was still available. He did, and got the part, and Sam very quickly had a hell of a cast on his hands.

The only problem for me was that my leg and foot were in a walking cast and I was still using crutches much of the time—something we couldn't adapt to the character. I would just have to bite the bullet and endure the searing pain when I walked during each performance. I appeared in only acts 1 and 3, so I iced my leg during the entirety of act 2.

Because they made me groggy, I couldn't take my pain pills until after the show each evening. So I would have them laid out and ready for me on my makeup table following each performance, and I would pray like hell that the audience wouldn't want too many curtain calls. Two performances in a day were absolutely out of the question, and Sam and the play's producers accepted my inability to perform in weekend matinees. When Sean announced that if *I* wasn't doing matinees, then neither would he perform on weekend afternoons, things got a little tense for a time, but the show remained a success even without the matinees.

I was surprised when Sam limited his direction to stage placement. He'd move each of us where he wanted us, then let us do our thing. "I want you, Nick, to be down to here for this one line you have to say. That's all the limitation I'll put on it." I tussled with that, because I didn't know how to get down there. If you get downstage and you don't know why you're supposed to be there, you can feel really naked.

Despite his unfounded worry that his talents didn't match those of the rest of us, Woody virtually stole every performance as a clueless taxi driver; Cheech Marin's *mejicano* sidekick shtick made audiences roar as well, and although my character Earl Moss wasn't every theatergoer's cup of tea, my grunting and slouching were well received.

By the end of our short run, my leg and foot were still killing me but I could also claim that special euphoria that comes when a group of people who care about each other collectively pull off something special. My return to the stage after thirty years reminded me how much I had loved it long ago, and it reminded me how much the stage remains the place where an actor foremost practices his art. I had come a long way.

In 2002, I had set aside alcohol and cocaine; my pneumonia was long gone, and even my slow-healing leg was finally on the mend. I had weathered the loss of my mother, although her absence was something I still felt every day. My sixteen-year-old son, Brawley, remained my life's greatest joy, and watching him grow was something I loved to do at very close range.

Neil Jordan, the Irish director of such fine films as *The Crying Game, Michael Collins,* and *The End of the Affair,* had offered me the lead in a film he had written called *The Good Thief,* based on a 1956 French film called *Bob le flambeur,* about an aging gambler who, with the help of a team that includes a young Russian prostitute, is about to risk everything on a spectacular casino heist while under the watchful eye of a policeman who might just choose to save his longtime opponent rather than arrest him.

Exquisitely shot on the French Riviera by cinematographer Chris Menges, the film is seductively stylish, intense, complex, and filled with excellent performances. I loved playing the role of Bob Montagnet, a brilliant gambler and thief who is also addicted to heroin. In order to portray Bob convincingly, I chose to become him in as many ways as I could—including using a bit of heroin during our eight-week shoot.

The decision made sense to me, and I never felt out of control. Although the film was a box-office failure, audiences and critics applauded it. I felt free throughout the shoot—unhindered and liberated to play the hell out of the role—and I discontinued the heroin as soon as our France and Italy shoots were complete.

Playing the role of the young prostitute was nineteen-year-old Nutsa Kukhianidze, who was from the city of Tbilisi in Georgia, which had been independent from the Soviet Union for a full decade by the time we made the film. Nutsa was from a prominent Georgian family; her grandfather owned all the movie theaters in the country, and so, of course, when the film was released internationally, we scheduled a press tour to Georgia to help make the most of the huge interest Nutsa's role in the film had generated.

But Georgia resembled the Wild West in the spring of 2003 and the moment our plane landed Nutsa's father-in-law stepped up and said, "Nick, these will be your nine bodyguards." And I said, "What? I don't have bodyguards." I knew this was going to be a film junket like no other. We raced from the airport in a multicar caravan, running red lights as we went. I had brought Brawley along with me on the short trip, and he was as astounded as I was when one of the thugs assigned to protect me explained that the cops we saw stopping cars everywhere along our route were actually robbers, simply men doing their everyday thievery.

The American ambassador to Georgia met us at the Holiday Inn where we would be staying—a short, fat American guy in a suit, surrounded by ten marines with arms nineteen inches around cradling M15s. I wondered how much protection they really offered him when I asked if we could visit the house where Stalin had been born and was very quickly told, "No. It's too dangerous."

"Okay," I said, as calmly as I could, "then what are we going to do?"

"We're going for a picnic up in the mountains," was

the answer I got from my bodyguards—so off we went. But during the picnic, out came the vodka, and they all got drunk as shit. Getting drunk made them want to pull out their Glocks, of course, with which they played a game by seeing who could shoot the most bottles. And they just couldn't hit anything.

Always up for an adventure, I said, "Let me have a try," and they were instantly accommodating. *Poom, poom, poom, poom, poom!* I took five quick shots and shattered five bottles, and my guys were *very* impressed. "What war were you in? What war were you in?" they asked, and I simply smiled and told them it wasn't a war. I was in the movies, I said. They nodded appreciatively.

On the way back to the hotel, a couple of members of my Georgian entourage—who apparently were related to Nutsa somehow—asked if I wanted to get a pain shot. I didn't know what they were talking about, but when one of them asked a second time, I said, "A pain shot? Sure. I could use one."

So, before long, Brawley went to his hotel room, and I was in mine, watching as a guy named Alexander was seated on the couch, tying up, and about to insert a needle into his vein. His pal Malkhaz tied off my arm and asked, "You do this before?"

I said, "Yes. But it's never looked like that." The

syringes contained something that was crystal clear, and all the heroin I'd ever seen was like tar. I was about to back out because this was obviously pure heroin, but just as I began to say no, Alexander fell to the floor. *Boom!* He was out. Malkhaz looked at his friend but wasn't concerned. He emptied his syringe into me, pulled it out, and in about two seconds, *boom!* I was out, too.

I learned some hours later that I turned blue-black during the fifteen minutes or so Malkhaz worked to revive me. Then, all of a sudden, I went, "*Ughhh, huh,*" and came back to life. Alexander was still lying on the floor when Malkhaz ran to get Brawley, and I remember him loudly instructing him, "Brawley, do *not* let your father fall asleep! Keep him walking. All night if you need."

Brawley wanted to know what had happened and I told him I didn't know, but that evidently someone had tried to kill us. I kept repeating those words—someone had tried to kill us—as we watched Malkhaz pulling Alexander's arm over his shoulder and hauling him out of the room en route to a hospital.

The next day, from up on the floor where my room was located, I could look down and see the preparations for the scheduled press conference. The bar and tables of food, the special tent that had been erected, and all the assembled media. But there was no way I was going to go down if someone was trying to kill us. I could see Alexander and Malkhaz looking up at me, motioning for me to join them—but I wouldn't do it. I was spooked.

They finally came up to the room, knocked on the door, and pleaded, "Look, Nick, you got to come down, no matter what. What happened yesterday not happening again. Not happening again. You got to come down because we promise a lot. We have . . . obligations."

I finally relented and went down and did my duty, and the press event went off as planned. I felt safer, somehow, in young Nutsa's presence. Her "cousins" Alexander and Malkhaz repeatedly assured me that there would be no more injections, and Brawley and I ultimately flew out of Georgia and home without any more pain relief or excitement.

Beginning back in my early years, when my mother would give me a "vitamin" to get me energized to go to school, I had consumed drugs or alcohol as part of my everyday experience. Much later in life, I became deeply interested in alternative medicine and the use of human growth hormone and dietary supplementation of many kinds. I had always struggled to be at ease in my own skin and to relax and simply accept what came my way. So it wasn't surprising that in the new century a substance that was readily available at health-food stores called gamma hydroxybutyric acid captured my attention.

Commonly known as GHB, it's a naturally occurring neurotransmitter that can also be synthetically produced in labs. Chemically closely related to GABA, it acts on both the GABA receptor and on the GHB receptor in the brain, where it can induce relaxation, mild euphoria, pain relief, and enhanced libido, as well as increasing growth hormone levels throughout the body. It was not considered a drug. It was an underground medication and aboveground commercial product.

In the late 1990s, GHB was entirely legal virtually everywhere, and my doctor prescribed it as a nightly sleep medication, which I used successfully for four years—sleeping much more soundly and deeply than I otherwise could. GHB was used medically as a general anesthetic and as a treatment for cataplexy, narcolepsy, and alcoholism. But the problem with GHB is that it is very dose specific, affecting everyone in diverse ways, and it is an incredibly easy substance to abuse.

I began to use it not only for sleep but also to help me relax and feel euphoric, to maintain my human growth hormone levels, and as an analgesic to reduce muscle pain during long and vigorous workouts. You don't feel the pain of tearing down the muscles when you work out for six hours. It adds a little euphoria. That's why it was in all the protein powders. Early in the new century, I wasn't drinking, wasn't doing coke or pot or other recreational drugs, but I began to increase my daily intake of GHB significantly.

The media had increasingly begun to refer to it as the "date-rape" drug, because some men were combining it with other drugs and pouring it into the beverages of women they hoped to take advantage of. The women would be so groggy that they could be sexually abused without fighting back or remembering what had happened to them the next day. If I had too much, I would fall deeply asleep in inappropriate places. Like park benches. Like cars.

On September 11, 2002, I had done something I often did—take GHB prior to going to the gym for a long workout. A strong dose made me feel great, yet I knew that I was dependent on it, knew that I was repeating with GHB the addictive cycle I'd been in with other substances in the past, and I was determined to get off it.

I knew there was a nooner Alcoholics Anonymous meeting at a nearby church, and I drove there and parked. I sat in the car and watched friends and strangers go into the church one by one, but I kept talking myself out of doing the same. I was just too fucked up to go to the meeting, I thought. Well, that's when you're supposed to go in. So what did I do?

Instead of simply leaving and driving the back roads home, for some reason I decided I'd take the direct route down the PCH, the Pacific Coast Highway. The highway was busy at midday, and all was well—or at least I thought it was—until I realized I had driven right past the turn-off to my house and I had no idea where I was going. I'm told six different drivers had called 911 to report that a big sedan was weaving on the wrong side of the road.

The California Highway Patrol dispatched a couple of cars to herd my car to the side of the road before I killed anyone or injured myself. I remember that before the first patrolman walked up to the car, I felt a sense of profound relief. I needed help.

I was a mess and the patrolmen, of course, presumed I had been drinking. I hadn't had a drop to drink in a long time. I knew that New York and Los Angeles were the only jurisdictions in the country that had just started testing for GHB, but it was so new, I presumed I wasn't in too much trouble. I was euphoric enough, in fact, that nothing really concerned me. They had me in the police station and I was feeling no pain. I mean, the police wrote things like, "He was drooling," and I'm sure I was. There was a paparazzo holding a camera over the fence, shooting photographs of me from the trailer park near the station. Someone took that crazy booking photograph that went instantly viral world-wide—my hair wild, my expression unsettling, and the overall effect making me look like an asylum inmate out for a lark in his flower-print Hawaiian shirt.

In 1992, *People* magazine had named me the sexiest man alive, and now, ten years later, I looked to all the world like a madman—and I couldn't be sure which of the two kinds of notoriety was worse. Yet that was of little concern that September. When I was released on bail a few hours later, I was cogent enough to call my lawyer and make some immediate plans. I made a call to a renowned East Coast psychiatric institution known for its addictions program, where I was told I could be admitted immediately. So I booked a private jet for the following day, then sat down with Brawley to talk.

He was sixteen by then, and still living with Vicki Lewis and me. He had a sound understanding of GHB, the ways in which it was beneficial to me, the drug's dangers, my physiological predisposition toward addiction, and the fact that I'd known for a while that I needed to get off it completely. There was a possibility that I would go into withdrawal, I told him, adding that a hospital dedicated to helping patients overcome addictions to a variety of substances would be the very best place for me if that occurred. He was supportive and resolved to keep up his studies with his tutor and the several other friends who were currently living and studying on our compound.

But when I reached the hospital and we began to discuss a treatment plan, I quickly learned that GHB was not something the hospital staff had experience with. In fact, the first thing they did was to investigate it on a government website, then inform me that withdrawing entirely and successfully would probably take two years, and that I would likely die in the meantime. To be honest, I knew lots more about GHB than anyone on the hospital's staff did, but they had addiction-recovery expertise that I really needed. So I stayed, and easily weaned myself off GHB, then flew home thirty days after being released. I was a renewed and fortunate man. My old identity had worn me out and I was grateful to have freed myself from its grasp. It was time for reinvention and reentry into the world.

The perfect opportunity for reinvention arrived in 2003 when I took a call from Terry George, the Irish screenwriter and director who had been imprisoned in the late 1970s in Northern Ireland's notorious Long

Kesh Prison for allegedly antigovernment activities as a member of the Irish Republican Army. In the years since, he had made a name for himself writing and directing films like *In the Name of the Father, Some Mother's Son, The Boxer,* and *A Bright Shining Lie*—pictures with a political consciousness and fiercely left-leaning point of view. I didn't know Terry, but I knew his reputation and I wanted to hear what was on his mind.

"You know, Nick," he said during our first conversation, "there are some films we do for money. There are some films we do for art. And then there are films we do because they just might kill us. And that's why you've got to do this with me."

"Holy shit," I responded—already halfway in after hearing a pitch like that.

"Well, it's genocide. You'll get the script. It's not a huge role but it's a significant role. Read it. That's why I'm doing it. I have to. And Don Cheadle is doing it."

I immediately liked Terry's style. He seemed like a straight-ahead kind of guy, someone who approached things a lot like I did, I suspected, and he didn't appear to be shy about anything. As soon as I read the script, I was committed as well.

The Rwandan genocide was the 1994 mass slaughter of African Tutsi tribespeople in Rwanda by members of the Hutu-majority government. Nearly a million Rwandans were killed between April and July of that year—almost 70 percent of all Tutsis and fully 20 percent of the country's total population. The widespread slaughter only ended when the Tutsi-backed and heavily armed Rwandan Patriotic Front took control of the country, and an estimated two million Rwandans, mostly Hutus, were displaced and became refugees.

In the film, whose screenplay was closely based on actual events, Paul Rusesabagina, played by Don Cheadle, is the manager of a Sabena airlines–owned hotel. He is Hutu, but his wife is Tutsi, and as the political situation in the country worsens following the assassination of the president, Paul and his family observe as neighbors are killed in the ethnic violence. Paul bribes officials with money and alcohol, hoping to keep his family safe, but when civil war breaks out Paul barely secures their safety by bringing them to the hotel. Don Cheadle is really powerful in the film. He's a solid actor. Very intellectual and savvy; he knows what he's doing and why he's doing it.

I played the Canadian Colonel Oliver, head of the United Nations peacekeeping forces in Rwanda—a character based on Canadian lieutenant-general Roméo Dallaire, whose hands were tied because he and his forces were forbidden to intervene in the bloodshed.

In a last-ditch effort to save the refugees, Paul first pleads with a Rwandan Hutu army general, then blackmails him with threats that he will be tried as a war criminal. Paul, his family, and other refugees at the hotel are finally able to leave in a UN convoy with Colonel Oliver's help, traveling through hundreds of thousands of fleeing refugees to reach safety behind Tutsi rebel lines. There is precious little that Oliver can do, but he is determined to help a few people survive, at least.

I knew from the first conversation I had with Terry that my part was a small one, but the power of the role of Oliver is that he is utterly helpless against what is going on. Oliver's powerlessness, his inability to stop hundreds of thousands of people from being chopped to death with machetes, is the key to the role, and I played the part mindful of the fact that the real UN commander, Dallaire, went home to Canada in the late summer of 1994, spiraled into a deep alcoholic depression, and attempted suicide several times. He had severe post-traumatic stress syndrome and in June of 2000, he was found in a semi-coma state under a park bench in Toronto.

Although there was that small United Nations presence in Rwanda, the reality is that the West utterly ignored the genocide. President Bill Clinton was adamant about not getting involved in Rwanda and the rest of the Western world turned its back as well. Hell was allowed to take hold on earth for a time—a truth that remains difficult to address, and the reason why, like Terry, I *had* to do the film.

I appreciated Terry's courage in bringing the horrific story to the screen, something that was a huge challenge at every turn. "It's simple: African lives are not seen as being as valuable as the lives of Europeans or Americans," he commented when he and other producers of *Hotel Rwanda* partnered with the United Nations Foundation to create the International Fund for Rwanda, which supported and still supports Rwandan survivors. "The simple goal of the film," he said, ". . . is to help redress this terrible devastation."

The wonderful British actress Sophie Okonedo, who is half Nigerian, powerfully plays Paul Rusesabagina's wife, Tatiana, in the film, a role for which she was nominated for an Academy Award. We filmed both in Rwanda itself and in South Africa, and it was fantastic to get to see some of Africa—a place where I'd never been—through the eyes of someone like Sophie, whose roots are there.

She and I got to know each other well, and it was fascinating that every time we went out to dinner during our time in South Africa we would be surrounded by people who were eager to hear about the world's opinion of their country more than a decade after apartheid had ended. Ironically, strangely, South Africa had held its first universal democratic elections and Nelson Mandela became president in the same year as the Rwandan genocide occurred, and people were both very proud and curious about the world's reaction.

We often would sit and talk with hope-filled young black South Africans until the restaurants finally closed at two in the morning. The conversations were always animated and I wanted these people I spoke with to know that, yes, the world was very aware of how dramatically different their history had been from what had occurred in Rwanda. "Look, you guys were able to do something remarkable," I said time and again. "In a radical, white-supremacist world, you were able to show the world how people *can* move forward ethically without bloodshed. I mean, you're the example," I wanted them to know, "that tells the world we *can* all get along."

Chapter 17
Sophie

Ben Stiller called me in 2005 and announced, "You know, Nick, we should work together." I'd met Ben several times before, and I knew his parents, the renowned actors and comedians Jerry Stiller and Anne Meara. Over the many months that followed, Ben and I played with a number of ideas, but nothing ever really took shape.

Then, late in 2006, Ben invited me to a Los Angeles read-through of a script he had cowritten that satirized epic Vietnam War films like *Apocalypse Now* and *Platoon*. The gathering would only include actors, he said, because he feared that no studio heads would go near a project like the one he wanted to produce, direct, and star in. "I don't know if anybody will accept it," Ben told me. "So, we're just going to read it. It'll just be a bunch of actors, and we'll just read it. It's called *Tropic Thunder*. You would play Four Leaf Tayback, this vet turned writer who has created this script based on his outrageous experiences in Vietnam, except that he was never actually there. Oh, and he has no hands."

"Okay," I said—always intrigued by a role in which I would be handless!

My assistant at the time, and someone with whom I'd worked for many years, was a great local kid in his thirties named Greg Shapiro, and although Greg was far too young to remember Vietnam, the idea for the film interested him and he wanted to accompany me to the read-through. I said sure, and as we prepared to drive into town, I gathered a big oxygen bottle with valves, plastic tubes, and a nasal cannula to take to the reading with me.

"Jesus, Nick," Greg said when he saw my props. "You're really going to walk in there with oxygen, for Christ's sake? You're nuts."

"Yes, I am nuts," I told him. "You know that." I thought it would be funny—and it turned out that it was; old Four Leaf Tayback was exactly the kind of guy who'd be puffing pure oxygen by now. Well, as soon as we got in the room I realized that it was kind of a setup, because it wasn't just about a dozen actors, all seated around a huge table, there was also the head of Disney Studios, whom Ben had enlisted to come listen and offer an opinion about whether something as outrageous as *Tropic Thunder* could actually get funded and produced.

Sure enough, the idea was so far out there that Ben wanted Robert Downey Jr. to wear *blackface* as he played a character that lampooned hyper-intense Method actors. So we went through the reading, and it evidently went off with a big bang, because it wasn't long after that Ben got his financing and we were scheduled to start shooting in Kauai in July 2007.

Ben's fertile brain had imagined a Vietnam War film that badly derails because of the giant egos of everyone involved. Stiller was scheduled to play Tugg Speedman, an aging action hero; Jack Black would portray a drug-addicted comic taking on his first serious film. Robert Downey Jr. would be one of the world's most awarded actors, the kind who gets utterly lost in every role—including, in this case, appearing in blackface. Downey did not know how that would go over. In fact, it was a discussion right up to shooting. Robert, on the first day of filming, was putting makeup on and wondering how deep the shade should be, what was acceptable or what was going to be *Amos 'n' Andy.* I said, "Don't worry, you'll make it work." And Downey did, you know. He put it together with care.

Later in the plot, when everything is about to go to hell due to the misbehaving actors, the "film's" director, played by Steve Coogan, takes the very questionable advice of hook-handed Four Leaf Tayback—me—and air-drops the actors into the jungle, hoping that something filmable will ensue. But when they happen onto a heroin producers' camp, it takes the "soldiers" a ridiculous amount of time to realize that the bullets, and the danger, are real.

Ben's big cast included a number of young comedic actors like Jack Black, Danny McBride, Bill Hader, and Matthew McConaughey. I was the designated old guy and I remember before we left for Hawaii that Jack, in particular, thought I was so ancient that he should regularly give me a hard time. But as a group of us sat down to dinner one evening in Santa Monica, Jack spotted singer David Crosby crossing the dining room of the restaurant where we were eating, and I heard him turn to someone, pointing out David and whispering that he was a "legend."

With that, I got up and walked over to David to say hello. We gave each other a big hug, and I told him he looked great. Jack was fucking *impressed,* to say the least, that an old geezer like me knew someone like David, and finally I became an acceptable acting companion in Jack's eyes.

My role in the film wasn't a major one, but Ben wanted me to be on set throughout the shoot on Kauai, so off I went at the start of principal photography. The whole scene on the island was craziness, with a million moving parts and people. This was clearly going to be a movie that would take a while to make. When you shoot a picture that lampoons an epic war film, you pretty much have to make an epic picture yourself, complete with helicopters, and bombers, and pyrotechnics of every kind.

As directed by Ben, we weren't playing comedy. In fact, he wanted us to play the script as straight-up as possible—just as real as we could. From Ben's perspective, one that made sense to me, if you lay a joke on top of the action, you're commenting on it. But if the writing is right, it's funny in itself, and you don't need to ham it up to make the joke land. I wasn't goofing around, in other words, playing some weirdo with two hooks instead of hands; I *was* a guy with two hooks. In the end, Tayback is proven to be a total phony. His hooks are just a cover, and, of course, he still has both of his hands—and that proved to be funny, too.

The crew was composed of ancient guys like me whom I'd worked with on films forever, and they were loving this one. "Man, what a cozy job this is," I kept hearing. "I don't care if we go over by a year. I could lie back in Kauai forever." The slow pace was fine with me, too, and sometimes I went for two or three weeks between days when we filmed a scene in which I appeared.

Yet I repeatedly made sure Ben knew I had a deadline when I absolutely had to leave, and he always answered, "No problem." Just to be sure, I reminded him in front of his wife, Christine Taylor, and that time they both assured me that, yes, they knew I *had* to be home in Malibu again in time for the birth of my daughter.

Flash back to five years before: I'd talked my assistant Patti into joining me in taking a Pilates class at a nearby studio. Patti committed, and we went several afternoons a week, and Clytie Lane, the class's young English instructor, got me into the best shape of my life. Truly. She would work with me during two-hour sessions four days a week; in the beginning Clytie was simply my Pilates coach, and then, over time, she became something more.

Clytie eventually moved to my place near Zuma Beach. I was healthy and happy, highly entertaining projects like *Tropic Thunder* were coming my way, and life was good. Then Clytie got pregnant and I was over the top with excitement. My son, Brawley, had been the biggest blessing of my life. We learned early on the new child was a girl, and the fact that I would be sixty-six when she was born didn't daunt me at all. I was *ready* to be a father once more and I was thrilled.

When Clytie was only a couple of weeks from her due date, I approached Ben on set in Kauai and reminded him that I had to leave. Christine was with him, and when she heard me, she turned and gave Ben a good whack. "Jesus Christ, Ben," she scolded, "haven't you finished Nick yet? You promised."

"Okay, okay," Ben sheepishly responded. "I promise. We'll get you done this week, Nick. We really will."

Christine turned to reassure me. "He's going to get you out this week, Nick. I'll make *sure* he does." And she did, and I was able to fly home in plenty of time.

It was early autumn and Clytie's pregnancy had gone smoothly. She had planned to deliver the baby at home—a water birth that would be attended by only three midwives and me. Brawley had been born in a hospital, where I waited in one of those expectant-father rooms until he arrived, but this time I would be very much a part of the action, and I wanted it no other way. As a former Pilates instructor, Clytie remained in great shape, and she was only thirty-eight, so it was hard to imagine that anything could go wrong.

On the morning of October 3, Clytie's water broke, and it was about to be showtime. We called the midwives, but after conferring with Clytie by phone, everyone agreed that they wouldn't arrive until her labor was truly under way. Clytie rested, and I got the birthing tub ready and was like a kid who couldn't wait for Christmas morning.

It seemed like forever, but in actuality, it was only a few hours later when the midwives arrived and one of them suggested that I get into the tub to help Clytie push. She nestled her back against my chest; we breathed together and then followed the midwife's instructions for Clytie to push back against me and downward.

Clytie pushed, then pushed harder, and then our extraordinary little Sophie emerged into the warm and welcoming water. She floated up, and when her head rose above the water's surface she took her first breaths and said hello to her two adoring parents. It was an extraordinary moment—a true meeting. This beautiful little creature was unique and our love for her was instantaneous and powerful.

The midwife helped position Sophie on Clytie's chest

and I continued to hold them—*two* of them now—against my own. We rested without anyone speaking for almost an hour. The room was still and felt sacred, and it was one of those rare experiences in which you know you're profoundly alive. Sophie Lane Nolte had just joined us, and I knew that I'd been reborn once again as well.

From the moment of her birth, Sophie's singular and adventurous spirit was obvious. Her father was an old guy who still loved new experiences and challenges of every kind, and her mom became a dedicated member of the Hare Krishna movement, and a talented kirtan singer. Clytie often hosted events at one of the houses on our property, and Sophie was steeped very early on in both an ancient spiritual tradition and my love of the natural world.

Whenever I could, I took her to the beach, to fields and forests, and she was often in a pack on my chest—facing forward and taking in all the world she encountered. I remember hiking with her outside Sedona and carrying her in a pack like that. As I climbed up over boulders to reach a challenging summit, sometimes her face was little more than an inch away from the rock, but she never turned away or was afraid. Through the years, I've watched her on our massive tree swing at the house, charging up and just letting loose. She was born with a combination of natural physicality and fearlessness that makes her want to push for more. Yes. She, like me, will push it.

I had been married three times, and three times those forever-after relationships had collapsed. This time, I was devoted to Clytie but we chose not to marry, and that was fine with me. Times had changed, I was certain, since back when I was a child and marriages tended to endure—regardless of whether couples remained in love.

What was most important, I now believed, was for people to concentrate on their relationships with their children, and for men and women to better understand that being a parent is the most important job you will ever have. Your responsibility to love and protect your child is the work you offer the world. Nothing else matters as much, least of all whether you're entirely in love with or compatible with your child's mother or father.

The world is in need of a children's bill of rights—a way for all of us to understand how precious our children are and how nothing matters as much as lovingly nurturing them into adulthood. That was something I had grown to deeply understand during the first twenty-one years of Brawley's life, and now that he had

a tiny sister, it was something I knew even more profoundly.

On October 3, 2007, the day of her birth, I began
my most important work of helping little Sophie travel
as high and as far as she could, kept aloft and safe by
her family's love.

Chapter 18
Graves Condition

A little more than a year before Sophie was born, we were about to begin filming *Pride and Glory,* a cop film set in New York and written and directed by Gavin O'Connor, whose father had been an NYPD captain himself. At a read-through of the script before we began shooting, we were joined by the young actor Edward Norton—almost thirty years my junior—who was playing the picture's lead.

I had met Ed at the Academy Awards ceremony in Los Angeles when both of us were nominated for best actor about eight years earlier—him for *American History X,* in which he portrays a reformed neo-Nazi, and me for my role in *Affliction.* This time around, he would be playing my son in the new police drama, but I was put off at the read-through by the way he kept telling several of us how we should play our characters. After I'd read one of the police captain's speeches, Ed announced, "Oh, we can't say anything like that. No father talks to his son like that."

"I beg your pardon," I replied.

"I said, no father talks like that to his son," he announced once more, his voice rising.

"Well, you are *fucking wrong*," I said. "I guess you don't have a father then, because my father sure as hell talked to me like that!"

"Well, it's just not playable for me," he responded dismissively.

I said, "You are not playable for me, either."

Ostensibly, the reading was finished. Gavin didn't try to smooth things over, so I simply left. Up in my hotel room, I sat and stewed and tried to figure out what I ought to do. Finally, with the kind of clarity that sometimes feels like a gift, I called Gavin, but it was late and he didn't answer his phone. "Gavin," I told his voice mail, "I hate to do this to you, man. I am really sorry for it. But listen, there is no way I am going to get through this film with Ed Norton. I'll slit his throat before we even get started. I mean, I can give you a good replacement for me. Jon Voight would be great. You're going to have to leap on the change quickly because you're starting in three weeks." And with that, I was out of there. They hired Voight and I didn't have to kill anyone.

In the years between my brief meeting with Edward Norton at the Academy Awards and my original casting as his father in *Pride and Glory,* I had gone from being the kind of actor who is basically only offered leading roles to someone who now was primarily considered for films in which I would play a grizzled old guy of some kind—a father or grandfather or goofy uncle or something. And that was okay. It was an inevitable part of aging, I presumed, and, as always, it was the quality of the script and the meatiness of the character that continued to interest me, not the size of my role.

When *Pride and Glory* premiered in 2008—with Jon Voight playing Captain Francis Tierney and Ed Norton playing his son—the film struggled both critically and financially, but I didn't take any pleasure in that. *Tropic Thunder,* on the other hand—the movie that Ben Stiller had worried was too out-there to get made—became a huge hit when it was released in the summer of 2008. The movie grossed $188 million worldwide and I was happy for Ben and company, but I was focused instead on beautiful little Sophie at that point and on the delights and complexities of becoming a father for the second time at age sixty-six.

———

Gavin O'Connor might have decided never to have anything to do with me again—and if he had I would have accepted his response, because I stuck by my decision to leave *Pride and Glory*. The film's production company, I noticed at the time, wove a story about my leaving because of the flare-up of an old knee injury—and I didn't care. It would have been utterly fine with me if they had cited "creative differences" between Ed Norton and me—it just didn't matter.

Yet it was cool that instead of being pissed off at me, Gavin stayed in close touch. He kept my message telling him I had to leave the film to avoid killing Ed Norton on his phone, and occasionally he would play it for me for fun. And he wanted to talk regularly, too, as he and his writing partner Cliff Dorfman began to conceptualize a new film. Gavin is an exhaustive kind of filmmaker. He researches and researches, casts, rewrites. I was told they were writing the father character specifically for me.

The guy they were creating was an aging father, too, and when Gavin finally let me read their completed screenplay, I was blown away. It was just brilliant. I knew it was excellent material right away. I wanted in.

Warrior is about an ex-marine, Tommy Conlon, played by Tom Hardy, who returns from the war in

Iraq to ask his estranged father to help him train for the biggest event in mixed martial arts history. Tommy's brother, an ex-fighter turned teacher, played by Joel Edgerton, also returns to the cage in a desperate bid to save his family from losing their home. With the help of his father—a once-terribly-abusive recovering alcoholic—Tommy is pitted against his brother in the event final, and, as they fight, the two brothers face their childhoods, their father, and the forces that long ago pulled them apart.

My character, the boys' father, Paddy Conlon, is a supporting part, yes, but it's a powerful role, and I was thrilled to play it—and to work under Gavin's direction at last. Neither son fully wants to reconcile with his father, and my character's terrible guilt, isolation, and pain are almost impossible for him to bear and he begins to drink again in despair.

It's a very powerful story—one that includes some redemption, too—but I wasn't thrilled with the MMA fighting. I wasn't a fan, I didn't watch too much of it, and it looked awful brutal to me. I hoped Gavin would consider a rewrite that would make both sons boxers instead.

"I know it's ugly and violent," Gavin responded, "but you've really got to find out what it's about. Go to some of the matches, meet some fighters, meet their parents, their girlfriends, see their life. And you'll see it's not about violence." And he was right, I ultimately discovered. The violence inside the cage is as brutally real as it can be—but the men and women who become MMA fighters, I came to understand, are seeking a sense of purpose in their lives, self-respect, and the opportunity to provide for their families.

Gavin was up-front in telling me that he had based several elements of Paddy Conlon's character on my own life. My reaction was to embrace it. I had never been silent about my own addictions, and playing the role of Paddy helped me further explore and come to understand who I am. I had firsthand experience with addictions—how destructive they are and how difficult they are to overcome—and I appreciated Gavin's belief in me as an actor. He told the press when *Warrior* premiered that he hoped my role as Paddy would remind both the industry and filmgoers of the kind of work of which I was capable, work that I'd been doing for decades. Gavin said, "I hope this brings him back and gets him the recognition he deserves as a national treasure." I don't know about all that, but coming from Gavin, I'll take it.

I got along very well with Tom Hardy. He's a brilliant actor. He likes to tell tall tales as much as I do. He'll give you a story that's full of shit. Once he claimed he was a low-class Englishman, yet he actually comes from extreme wealth. He told me, "My dad, man, I used to beat the shit out of him outside of the house. I'd just bash his head into the car, you know." That was likely all the testosterone talking. I replied, "Well, Tom, I couldn't reach my dad to hit him. He was six foot six. All I'd get was air." So I bullshitted him back.

It was one of the few times we would hang out, as I thought it best that I didn't socialize much with Joel and Tom off-camera. Gavin thought that was right because when actors fraternize between takes, all the work you do preparing for the on-screen relationship is ruined. All the tension must be rebuilt. And that whole film was built on the tension between us three.

Warrior was one of those pictures that had a wide range of responses from critics when it was released in September 2011. It was either "cathartic" and "beautiful," or a film with "a lunkhead plot." A few opinions fell somewhere in between, but the movie ultimately failed to earn back its budget. However, I was honored to receive my third Academy Award nomination for the role as Paddy Conlon.

I'd assumed that at age seventy-one, my days of receiving award nominations were long over. Thirty-five years before, I had received a Golden Globe nomination when I played a young boxer struggling to bond with his brother and his parents in *Rich Man, Poor Man*. My first Academy Award nomination had come fifteen years later for my role in *The Prince of Tides*, in which I played a man haunted by his upbringing and desperate to find a way to be the father he wants to be. I had been nominated for a second Academy best-actor award six years later for my role in *Affliction*, playing a man crippled by all that his father failed to offer him.

I'd won a number of awards in the U.S. and abroad over the years. But I figured I was too long in the tooth now. So I was truly surprised when the Academy nominated me for a best supporting actor Oscar for my role in *Warrior*.

I appreciated the recognition, yet I continued to believe that the idea of "best" when it came to acting was a very mistaken one, and I wasn't surprised when the winner that year was the wonderful Christopher Plummer, who won for his role in *Beginners*. The Academy voters preferred, in the end, a far more redemptive character than Paddy Conlon could be, yet at the end of *Warrior*, Paddy has much to still live for as well. And I knew in my own heart that some kinds of recognition are far more meaningful—and truly important—than others.

We shot *Warrior* in Pittsburgh, a city I'd gotten to know well over the years and liked a great deal. During the shoot, I befriended an ex–narcotics cop who was my driver and whom everyone knew as simply Jimmy from Pittsburgh. Jimmy was a poet and operated gyms for the city's underprivileged kids. He and I forged something special during our days together.

I remember getting a phone call from Jimmy one morning, and he sounded like a man with a plan. "First thing we got to do is this Saturday, we've got to go to the Steelers stadium at eight o'clock. There's a local campaign against gun violence and the leadership will run a scroll of all the people who have been shot with handguns in the city in the last five years. There are going to be about ten thousand people in the stadium. The mayor is going to talk, and then a priest will talk, and then I'm going to talk for about five minutes, and you're going to talk for twenty minutes about nonviolence."

I said, "Sounds good, Jimmy, let's do that."

Yet when I came down from my room that Saturday morning and met Jimmy in his car, he was visibly shaking and something clearly was very wrong. I said, "Are you going to tell me what the fuck's going on?"

"Yeah, some horrible events, and they're still going

on," he replied. "So far, since last night, three cops have been killed. They went through a door last night, and they walked in on a kid who had an AR-15 and an ammunition stash. He shot the first five through the door. The rest of the cops surrounded him, but he still won't surrender. This speech at the stadium has turned into a huge thing. Now it's going to be the governor, the cardinal, some bishops. I am still going to talk for five minutes and you are still going to talk for twenty and we will keep the crowd updated on the situation as we go."

I didn't respond with anything more than, "Okay," because this was fucking tragic. The murder of three cops was untenable. I was as shaken as Jimmy was, but somehow that day I found words about choosing cooperation and nonviolence to share with what must have been a hundred thousand people. Most of Pittsburgh was there.

It was one of those things that just empties the life and hope out of you. Fifteen kids were orphaned that night. They had been proud of their dads, but now their dads were gone forever. After the program, Jimmy suggested that he and I visit some precincts, to say hello and show our support, and as we did, we heard repeatedly that hundreds of surviving cops' kids were now terrified that they would lose *their* dads, too. Just seeing their dads in uniform freaked them out now.

"Well, bring them into work with you, for sure," I suggested to the cops with whom we spoke. And then I had an idea. "Let's get lots of kids, the kids who're scared and even some of the kids whose dads died last night, and let's get them into a station on National Take Your Child to Work Day. We'll get television reporters and cameras here, too, and we'll help the kids have some fun, if just for a minute or two."

Hundreds of children arrived at the precinct within a couple of hours, and every television station in the city filmed our impromptu afternoon. I just winged it, and Jimmy and his brothers in blue helped me pull off something none of us could have imagined doing. Black kids and white kids of every age joined us and we *did* have fun, goofing for the camera, sending the message that all of us have no choice but to care for each other as we fumble our way into the future.

Gavin was at home and he saw me on the TV with the kids. Everyone saw me on TV, and because I had a mug that lots of people recognized after thirty-six years in film, when I was walking down the street, the Pittsburgh bus drivers and cab drivers would stop and say, "Hey, Nick, need a ride?" They were appreciative. And it was one of the most memorable days of my life.

I hadn't appeared in a television series or movie since *Rich Man, Poor Man,* but by 2011, TV had emerged as the medium in which the best storytelling and acting were currently taking place. Shows like *Breaking Bad, Mad Men, The Shield, The Sopranos,* and *The Wire* were considered to have ushered in television's new "golden age," and it was an exciting time.

I certainly wasn't one of those actors who ever thought it was beneath me to appear on television, and when an opportunity arose for me to secure a recurring role in a series developed by the legendary writer-director David Milch, I leapt at it. Milch had cocreated *NYPD Blue* and was the creator of HBO's *Deadwood,* which many now consider the finest television drama ever produced. *Deadwood's* brilliance left many of us presuming that everything Milch touched would inevitably turn to gold.

It was Milch's next show for HBO that included a character who was right for me, he believed. This new series would be about a bunch of intersecting lives in the world of horse racing. Milch pitched me his whole concept for *Luck* when he came to see me that first day. He had it well in hand. My character was a much-traveled and guilt-ridden horse trainer named Walter Smith. Our ensemble cast would be anchored by

Dustin Hoffman in the lead role as an aging con who is released from prison as the series begins.

The cast of *Luck* was incredible. Hoffman was pretty relaxed. He'd stumble around in rehearsals, but when it was showtime, he would be right on point. When a scene flows naturally, that's the juice us actors live off. Anyone far enough along in this profession knows to just let it loose and trust the moment. Hoffman has that.

In order to get the show green-lit, Milch had had to agree to HBO's demand that director-producer Michael Mann would direct the first two episodes, so that Milch himself could focus entirely on the writing, but the two men clashed mightily right from the outset. On our very first day of shooting, I bumped into David outside my trailer, and he pointedly asked, "Nick, what do you think of this motherfucking cocksucker Michael Mann?"

And I answered, "Well, David, you know, I don't think I can afford to have an attitude about him because I've got to go and suit up, you know?"

"Oh, shit," David responded. "That's right, you're shooting. Oh, fuck. I'm sorry. I'll get the fuck out of here." And he was right. It wasn't good for me to see him so angry at the man who would be directing me. I knew what my immediate goal had to be, and that was simply to fully embody my character—and let David be the brilliant, brilliant writer he can be.

Despite the tension on set, we had the makings of a fine series. I watched the episodes, and they were excellent. Yet much of the drama was carried by the horses, and I knew we couldn't depend on the races themselves for our storylines time after time. During the same period we were filming, a horse fell, severely breaking its leg, and had to be put down. Then a second horse was injured and had to be euthanized during the shooting of the seventh episode.

HBO had renewed us for a second season already, but with the outcry from PETA and the unfortunate death of a *third* horse, HBO canceled the show. The agency that officially oversees animal welfare in film and on television is the American Humane Association. They had been working closely with us, but regardless, there are unforeseen accidents that can happen. It was not only tragic but a deeply disappointing and abrupt end to our show. But we were professionals, too, and we understood the complex dynamics that led to the decision.

In my seventies now, who knew if I'd ever return to television again? Acting is as big a gamble as horse racing is, and at least my time spent shooting at the Santa Anita racetrack led to a special reunion for me personally. When my high school football teammate and good friend Steve Priborski—a farrier working at the track whom I had met a million years before at Omaha's Benson High—heard that I was working on *Luck* and came over to say hello, the two of us were able to renew almost instantly one of those kinds of friendships that can survive the decades and just don't ever die. Deep friendships with people from outside of the industry can ground an actor profoundly. Equally valuable, but somehow always harder for me to keep up, are friendships I've developed inside the acting world. Luckily, the prospect of a great project creates enough pull to lure me out of hibernation and reconnect me with folks like Robert Redford.

Bob and I went way back—not as far back as Omaha, but we'd been working in the same small industry for many years and we had always respected each other. Just three years before, I'd said yes to a small role as Bob's character's old comrade and fellow aging radical in *The Company You Keep,* a political thriller he had directed and starred in. Although we're good friends, Bob and I have always approached our careers a bit differently.

Back when we were both represented by lawyer Gary Hendler, I remember Gary telling me that I needed to shape my career like Bob's. "He does a couple of studio movies and then gets to do one for himself," Gary said, as if to encourage me to do the same. And I laughed. "Gary, I'm doing one for myself now, and next I'm going to do one for myself, then after that I'll do another for myself, too," which pissed Gary off, but at least he understood my unwavering position on the matter.

When Bob wanted to talk with me about *A Walk in the Woods,* I went into his office in Santa Monica, where he asked, "Do you want to do it?" I answered, "I'd love to do it." And the deal was done. Bob had originally wanted to cast his dear friend Paul Newman in the role, but the timing had never been right and Paul had passed away before they could realize that dream. Now Bob wanted to hire a new writer, and he included me in the process. We met with several writers, had a couple of versions of the screenplay rewritten, then did a read-through. We really worked at it, and it took us about a year, during which Bob went off and did the film *All Is Lost.*

Bob is only five years older than me, so we're basically from the same generation, but in reality, he belongs to Newman's generation, in part because he started working in films very young and celebrity came early to him, and I was an unknown actor until my late thirties. Bob's generation wasn't quite as hip as mine was—or perhaps as wild—but he and I have always seemed to share similar principles.

When I act, I'm trying to create an archetype, a general feeling for audiences that allows them to experience something outside themselves when they watch me at work. It's much larger than me, and it's something I simply must do to survive. I don't know how to do anything else. I've played these archetypes for more than fifty years now. If I ever run out of stories that mean something to me, then I won't tell them anymore. But I have to risk making mistakes. Life is full of blunders, but they are our teachers. You pay attention, and you simply figure things out along the way.

That lesson, that truth that life isn't worth shit unless you're willing to take some risks, was something which seemed inherent to me in Bill Bryson's memoir *A Walk in the Woods*. Bob had recognized that element, too, and I remember his telling me that the biggest reason he bought the film rights was because no other book had made him laugh so hard in a very long time. Bryson told Bob to go ahead and do it, and have fun. With that blessing, Bob proceeded.

The book is the true story of Bryson's decision to hike the entire two-thousand-mile length of the Appalachian Trail, despite the fact that he's in his sixties and not much of an outdoorsman. His wife—played by Emma Thompson in the film—thinks he's crazy and insists that he find a companion to join him and help keep him alive, but all his friends are far too logical to join him, except for his old buddy Stephen Katz. Overweight, out of shape, and the kind of fellow who has always held his life together with nothing more than baling wire and a handful of luck, Katz was a character I knew I could have a very good time with.

In a way that seems quite real to me, Katz admires his friend Bill's literary and financial success as well as his stable and supportive marriage. Bryson, in turn, is drawn to Katz's freedom, his ability to live each day exactly as he chooses, his willingness—no, his *need*—to take significant risks. The two men respect each other, but they challenge each other, too, and each is a bit jealous of what the other has. Katz says, "Look at what you've got. You've got a home and a wife, a steady kind of thing." But Bryson feels stifled and prematurely *finished*. The two men represent a dynamic tension that almost all of us have to deal with daily—especially as we get older. And for me personally, no matter how attractive the settled and secure life appears sometimes, I've never been able to do the safe thing. Never. I've always done stupid things, or I've been brilliant. It's been one or the other.

One of the great pleasures of making *A Walk in the Woods* was that it got us out into nature. Bob and I were both too damn old to rough it and camp out, but we had a ball nonetheless. I try to spend as much time in the woods and fields as I can. I don't do well in cities, and that's why I've chosen to live in a secluded compound in Malibu for so long, one where I can spend as much time as I want hermiting in my big gardens, growing vegetables and eating food that's as fresh as it can be, getting my hands dirty and working up a good sweat. It's something that connects me to my childhood, of course, and the quiet, rural life has always kept me sane. Sane-ish.

I loved shooting on location up and down the Appalachian Trail, where the story takes place. I was in lousy shape—which was perfect because so is Katz. At the end of the day, we were beat. We were really roughed up from shooting the scenes. There was none of this movie stuff of "I'm going to my trailer"; there were no trailers. We were exposed to the elements all day. That took a while to get used to. We walked a lot. I replaced my hip right after the film to match my fake knee. I'm becoming bionic. Early sports injuries and years of ignoring my body's aches and pains had turned me into something of a geezer. But *A Walk in the Woods* is a geezer picture, of course, so all was well.

There is something about wildness that appeals to me. I'm enamored of the craziness that lies somewhere deep inside each of us, because we are each uniquely made. I like that, and it appeals to me to express the truth—onstage and in front of the camera—that inside each of us is a unique and wild entity. Each of us is part of a universe that is comprised of both the inescapable rules of physics and the infinite chaos of stellar explosions and imploding black holes.

But the universe gets along fine, despite its inherent absurdity. And we, as part of the universe, attempt to make the world we inhabit rational and coherent and predictable, when it's really highly random. Think about it for a moment: the universe says to us, "You get to live, but the catch is that you have to die." Who in the world would take a deal like that? Well, I believe each of us does.

Every one of us struggles to make life livable somehow, and my way of making my own life palatable has always been to just bite it on the ass, to take big risks, then find ways to either celebrate or survive them. I've always loved a Cervantes-inspired quote, one that I've often hung on the walls of my film-set trailers: "In order to attain the impossible, one must attempt the absurd." I've actually achieved the impossible a time or two—at least in some deep part of me I believe I have—and chaos has always followed me like a randy dog. I'm just as ridiculous as I can be sometimes, and that's why I was so drawn to a character like gruff and grizzled old Katz and his enthusiastic inclination to join his pal for a two-thousand-mile walk through the woods.

There is some irony in the fact that although I was determined as a kid never to study much in school, I've loved my opportunities to mentor young people over the years. Always a lousy student, I think I've been a pretty good teacher. And the truth is that I would never have gotten anywhere in this business if I hadn't been eager to learn from some wonderful mentors, too, legends like Kit Carson, Allen Dutton, Helen Langworthy, Alan Rudolph, Paul Mazursky, Mike Medavoy, and many, many others.

Some of my assistants over the years have primarily focused on helping me clerically or personally, and others have wanted to glean as much from me as they could about the wildly complex and unpredictable industry in which we work. Twenty years ago, when I met twenty-four-year-old Greg Shapiro, who had joined me as my assistant on the film *Mulholland Falls,* I asked him on the first day we worked together, "Do you have any idea what this is going to be like?"

"Well, I hope it's going to be everything!" he responded with a grin and great enthusiasm.

I liked his response, and I met it with some eagerness of my own. "Yes, exactly. And you know, in this first film I strongly suggest that you get experience in all these areas. Go through preparation, into production, as far as into casting and all of that as they will let us, and then work every day on the film. Don't focus on getting me cigarettes when I have a whim, or a shot of tequila, or whatever. Watch on the monitor all the scenes I'm doing, because we'll plot them out, and maybe there will be some things you catch. And then watch the dailies, too, and the next day you can tell me how the dailies were. Or, if there's something that really alarms you, call me, and I'll take a special look at them."

Greg dove in headfirst and did a terrific job, soaking up the facets of filmmaking like a sponge. After some time, he wanted to take the next steps for someone eager to make a career out of film, hoping I'd agree for us to form a production company called Kingsgate Films and start making our own movies together. I told him I was way too busy and focused on acting to head up that kind of effort, but when he insisted that he'd do all the work, I made sure he knew what he was getting into.

"Okay," I told him, "it will mean you're going to have to meet writers, established writers and up-and-coming writers, foreign writers, get a huge collection of stories, figure out what you want to say, and then, after the material's written, shape it into movie form and follow it all the way through to production, including hiring a director—at which point your work will only really get started." I looked at him hard. "To be a great producer, you'll have to be the core of all of this, the heart of this particular kind of storytelling. You. It will all depend on you."

Greg said, "Yes, Nick. That's what I want to do." So, off we went, with Greg initially working out of my property in Malibu for two years. Greg then recruited an ambitious young friend, Joel Lubin, who now is co-head of Creative Arts Agency's motion picture talent department, to join our company, and we soon got a deal with Fine Line/New Line and had an office on Santa Monica Boulevard in West Hollywood. That deal was a result of *Mother Night,* which was a Fine Line film. When that deal expired, we moved to Phoenix Pictures, which was Mike Medavoy's office. I had just done *The Thin Red Line* for Phoenix Pictures and Mike and I had been interconnected through the years, working on many films together all the way back from the *Heart Beat* days.

In the end, Greg and I produced five or six films together. Our first film was *Simpatico,* produced by my company Kingsgate Films, based on a Sam Shepard play, which starred me, Jeff Bridges, and Sharon Stone. Next came *Neverwas,* which was directed by a talented young fellow Greg connected with named Joshua Michael Stern.

I watched with pride as Greg built his repertoire with projects that both interested him and possessed real juice—even if they weren't big moneymakers— which is exactly what, beginning a long time ago, I had tried to convince him was important. Greg's impressive producing chops earned him an Academy Award in 2010 when *The Hurt Locker* was named best picture of the year. Then a few years thereafter, Greg had a new concept for a TV series that brought him, Josh Stern, and me back together.

Greg took his idea to Josh, hoping they could collaborate. But Josh was focused on his preparations to direct the 2013 biopic *Jobs,* starring Ashton Kutcher, and he turned the proposal down. When at last the time was right, the two spent a year creating the show, writing the pilot, and finding a home for it at Epix, a new premium cable channel.

Graves is an original television series in which I play a former president of the United States who sets out to undo the many wrongs of his administration, while dealing with the political ambitions of his wife, played by Sela Ward. The storyline that the former president's wife is running for the U.S. Senate is one that came from me. I didn't want the show to be built around stock kinds of characters who lack that "juice" that's so vital to a series. I wanted each one to have a strong arc and tension on their own. It was also important to me that Graves and his wife are partners of equal standing. The show is set in Santa Fe because it's a real place and it's *not* New York or L.A.—where so many shows are set—and because New Mexico is not only gorgeous but one of those states that offer tax incentives to encourage film and television production. We have a great cast and some fine writers, and I've enjoyed two epic seasons back in television again after *Luck* got very unlucky.

But more than that, at seventy-six I'm *starring* in *Graves*, and that's my great good fortune. Lots of actors my age, men and women alike, only are offered window-dressing kinds of roles, grandma or grandpa parts that are often very two-dimensional—characters who are either sweet and lovable old codgers or who are so damn ancient and mean that no one wants to come near them. In this case, I was offered a multifaceted character to play specifically because Greg Shapiro and Josh Stern imagined me at the center of a show like this.

Our several-month shoot in New Mexico during the winter and spring of 2016 was hard on me. I had a new titanium hip, as well as a new knee, and I was postponing laminectomy surgery on my back in order to get the first ten episodes shot. I was in constant and sometimes excruciating pain. To make matters worse, a complete set of dental implants that were on order weren't finished in time for the shoot, so I had to use dentures—appliances both my tireless assistant Denise and I despised as they inevitably wiggled their way out of my mouth and she would have to chase them back in.

But being in Santa Fe was a true pleasure, as always. The front-desk kid at the La Fonda hotel didn't quite know what to do when I asked him whether the hotel staff had ever found my father's wooden leg.

Graves has run for two successful seasons so far, and once again—despite my seventy-six years, or maybe just because of them—I received a Golden Globe nomination, for my performance in season one. Jacqueline Bisset made a guest appearance in season two, bringing back my boyish shyness from my younger days on *The Deep.* Her beauty still transcends, but who am I kidding? I'm ancient. Critics seemed to agree, commenting repeatedly about my getting damn old, one of them claiming, "Nolte's voice sounds as though he's just gargled with glass shards. Moreover, his physical appearance resembles a totaled car."

Big surprise! I was seventy-five and hurting. I looked and sounded like I was in *Graves* condition, pun intended, but it's something that happens to everyone if you stick around long enough. I had worked for over a full decade in regional theater, and then, beginning with "The Feather Farm" on *The Wonderful World of Disney,* I had appeared in *ninety-nine* credited roles in television programs, television series, and feature films between 1969 and 2017. I had been very busy telling stories, and I'd had an extraordinary run by anyone's measure.

By turns, I had been brilliant and had fallen flat on my face; I had become father to two tremendous children and they were both proud of and embarrassed by their dad. I had taken big risks along the way, and loved a number of women powerfully and sometimes poorly. I also could claim friends like Gerardo Resendiz, an immigrant from Mexico who for nearly forty years has been my carpenter, gardener, Rock of Gibraltar, and dear and steadfast friend.

Playing the role of a former president who looks back on his consequential life has encouraged me to do the same thing. In the second season, my character even writes his memoirs! I realize this is a new irony; all the times in which I have relied on my art form to help infuse my life with purpose and now the art mimics my real-life ponderings. Sometimes, these ponderings have brought a bit of pride; at other times I've winced, and even occasionally wished I could crawl into a hole. But regardless, my story will soon join all the tomes in my tree house library that have informed my journey. Among those books are the threadbare ones that saved me a lifetime ago in that little room in Phoenix.

At seventy-six, I really must begin to address the question of dying, and it's something I'm doing without undue fear because I've always had to face fear and the crippling anxieties it brings. Many of my contemporaries are gone by now, and I suspect I've got five years or so before I, too, get to head "elsewhere" to be rebellious and cause more glorious havoc.

When I reflect on all of the roles I've had—as a corn-fed Midwestern kid trying to make his parents proud, a football player, an actor, a lover, a father—it feels like it's a meaningless exercise unless it offers something to the present moment, to the present act in which I encounter myself and the world around me. Like it or not, I've led a public life, and reflection also inevitably rubs the public and private versions of me together in ways that are sometimes abrasive, yet at other times the two seem to meaningfully connect.

When you act, the audience or the camera puts you in a self-conscious place, a condition you must try to get over, even though you never can, and it's a condition that's related to death in some ways. You step over a line, and you have no idea what will follow, but you know you must take the step forward. No one can go backward.

As an actor, you become a student of people, and that process of observing them is, in a way, a psychological relief from having to live your own life. You may die five or six times onstage or on the screen, and you think it teaches you something about dying. But it isn't until mothers, fathers, friends start dying that you truly do begin to make sense of the way in which death rather miraculously gives meaning to life. So it's curious—an actor like me can portray a thousand men over a lifetime, but away from the lights and cameras, I've had nothing but my own personal experience to turn to, and real life, as I've written, has never been easy for me.

Yet here's the thing: it's a rare and precious opportunity to live profoundly in the moment—something that very few people get to do. It's an opportunity to give everything you've got to your imagination, and I'm one of those people who believe that imagination is reality. I don't make a distinction between unreal and real. I don't say that acting is not living. It is living! In fact, it's entirely possible that I am never more *truly* alive than in the moments and hours when I'm imagining and immersed in a character. I've believed for so long that *real life* causes me trouble that I failed to recognize that acting is conscious living at its most profound.

Whether onstage or in film, it's impossible to play a character who is exactly the same on two different days, just as our brains never return to precisely the same state twice—not ever. Acting and living are processes that require constant flexing, changing, growing, evolving. It's our nature as human beings to be adaptable and pliable, and to be self-aware and self-confident enough to let yourself come truly alive in your imagination is a tremendous feat. My mother would be proud that I gleaned that from her.

Yet you should acknowledge, I think, that you can't live in that state always and forever. And because you can't, you do your best to keep a sense of humor in your pocket, to stay in the present, to read and continue to learn, and to really love the people you love. You stay active in the moment—in the garden, walking in the woods, and constantly, if silently, chanting your gratitude for everything that you have and all that you've encountered during the years you've searched for yourself.

While I acknowledge that death will arrive for me before too many more years pass, I want to prepare for it without giving it too much conscious thought. We are all terminal cases, after all, and if you can still take breaths, you should feel lucky. I've had a wonderful time living, and I look forward to a good time dying. In the meantime, I hope to return to Santa Fe to film the third season of *Graves*, and to my renewed opportunity to imagine that I'm President Richard Graves again, letting all my life that I've lived 'til now help me step once more into that wonderful realm of imagination where I'm most at ease and at home.

And I'm sure I'll stop by the La Fonda again to see, damn it, if we can't finally find Dad's wooden leg.

Afterword

DIARY ENTRY FROM THE 1980s

He walks followed by his birthday, and facing his death day.

The dash hints at his end, eagerly awaited by historians who can thus officially close the parentheses.

The essential thing about him, and this is the essence of fame, is that he is between parentheses—he is not free.

This monumentalization of people, this freezing of life, is the terrible curse of the consciousness of fame.

Anybody with instinct destroys conventional fame and misleads his admirers and biographers by being unreliable and therefore unpleasant . . .

This gives him the possibility of looking instead of being looked at.

Acknowledgments

While drawing inside and out of the lines, many people kept my handwriting steady . . .

First off, I'd like to thank HarperCollins for its patience and vision. It took a lot longer than we thought, but by God, we did it! It also took a stellar staff to bring this to its polished and coherent state. At Harper-Collins I thank Liate Stehlik, our publisher; David Palmer, our production editor; Rich Aquan, the cover designer; Katherine Turro, the marketer; Heidi Richter, the publicist; and Victor Hendrickson, assistant general counsel. May Chen, our keen-eyed editor, was supportive every step of the way. Thankfully, she got my weirdo humor from the start. Gabrielle Keck, assistant editor, was a tenacious detail-wrangler.

Paul Mazursky may have initially encouraged me to

pen these stories, but his daughter Jill Mazursky followed through and made it seem possible. I have her to thank for connecting me to my literary agent, Ian Kleinert of Objective Entertainment—whose enthusiasm and steadiness saw us all the way to the end.

For the early forging of the book, I thank Guru Das and Mike Downs who listened deeply and gave me a leg up and Russell Martin for putting things in some semblance of order. Projects like this require a supreme amount of tenacity and vision, so thank goodness, Denise Hardy has those in spades, not to mention the strength to take on a difficult subject—me!

I thank my assistant, Briana Sandford, for showing up every day and getting me out of bed. And lastly, I thank my family: Nancy Nolte, Eric Berg, and Rebecca Linger, for being steadfast over the years and Clytie, Brawley, and Sophie, for being my inspiration.

HARPER LUXE

THE NEW LUXURY IN READING

We hope you enjoyed reading
our new, comfortable print size and found it
an experience you would like to repeat.

Well – you're in luck!

HarperLuxe offers the finest in fiction and
nonfiction books in this same larger print size and
paperback format. Light and easy to read, HarperLuxe
paperbacks are for book lovers who want to see
what they are reading without the strain.

For a full listing of titles and
new releases to come, please visit our website:

www.HarperLuxe.com